DIRECTORY OF SOCIAL CHANGE

MAY 2000

SCHOOL FUNDRAISING IN ENGLAND

A DIRECTORY OF SOCIAL CHANGE RESEARCH REPORT

—— SUPPORTED BY THE BARING FOUNDATION ——

Anne Mountfield ● **Nicola Eastwood**

Registered Charity No. 800517

Published by
The Directory of Social Change
24 Stephenson Way
London NW1 2DP
Tel: 020 7209 5151, fax: 020 7209 5049
e-mail: info@dsc.org.uk
from whom further copies and a full publications list are available.

The Directory of Social Change is a Registered Charity no. 800517

Copyright © Directory of Social Change 2000

All rights reserved. No part of this book may be stored in a retrieval system or reproduced in any form whatsoever without prior permission in writing from the publisher. This book is sold subject to the condition that it shall not, by way of trade or otherwise, be lent, re-sold, hired out or otherwise circulated without the publisher's prior permission in any form of binding or cover other than that in which it is published, and without a similar condition including this condition being imposed on the subsequent purchaser.

ISBN 1 900360 58 6

British Library Cataloguing in Publication Data
A catalogue record for this book is available from the British Library

Designed and typeset by Penny Drinkwater
Printed and bound by Antony Rowe, Chippenham

Other Directory of Social Change departments in London:
Courses and Conferences tel: 020 7209 4949
Charity Centre tel: 020 7209 1015
Research tel: 020 7209 4422
Finance and Administration tel: 020 7209 0902

Directory of Social Change Northern Office:
Federation House, Hope Street, Liverpool L1 9BW
Courses and Conferences tel: 0151 708 0117
Research tel: 0151 708 0136

The views expressed in this report are from a variety of sources and may not necessarily reflect those of the Directory of Social Change. Whilst every care is taken to provide accurate information, neither the publisher nor the authors undertake any liability for any error or omission.

This report was supported by the Baring Foundation.

CONTENTS

		Page
1	Executive Summary	5
2	Introduction	9
3	Survey Findings:	
	Primary Schools in England	19
	Secondary Schools in England	35
	Independent Schools in England	49
	Special Schools in England	59
	What the Teachers Said	69
4	Policy Issues and Proposals	75
	Index	79
	Acronyms, and Areas used in the survey	80

Acknowledgements

The Directory of Social Change wishes to acknowledge the kind support of the Baring Foundation of the research for this report, and the patience of successive Directors: David Carrington and Toby Johns.

Our sincere thanks go to over 1,000 busy headteachers of English primary, secondary, special and independent schools, all of whom took the time to complete and return our 8-page questionnaire, often adding lengthy personal comments that provided invaluable insights.

We also gratefully acknowledge the many other people who have been generous with time and advice.

About the authors

Anne Mountfield was, until 1999, the Assistant Director of the Directory of Social Change, and its Head of Publications. From 1990 to 1994 she was a senior researcher at the Directory of Social Change, specialising in education. She was a teacher for many years.

Publications include:
State Schools – A Suitable Case For Charity? Directory of Social Change 1991; *The Charitable Status Of Schools – What Needs To Be Done?* Directory of Social Change 1992; Charitable Funding And Fundraising In Schools –Time For A Closer Look? *Researching the Voluntary Sector* Charities Aid Foundation 1993; *School Fundraising – What You Need To Know* Directory of Social Change 1993; *A Guide To Fundraising For School Grounds* Learning Through Landscapes 1995; *The Education Funding Guide* Directory of Social Change 1995.

Nicola Eastwood, now a freelance researcher, worked for the Directory of Social Change from 1988 to 1992 and, with Mike Eastwood, established the Northern Office of the Directory of Social Change in 1988. She has been a school governor for nine years.

Publications include:
A Guide to Company Giving 2nd edition Directory of Social Change 1990; *A Guide to Grants for Individuals in Need* 3rd edition Directory of Social Change 1991; *The Sports Funding Guide* Directory of Social Change 1995; *The Youth Funding Guide* Directory of Social Change 1997.

Both will be authors of a new DSC publication for autumn 2000: *The Schools Funding Guide*

EXECUTIVE SUMMARY

This survey was carried out by the Directory of Social Change in 1999–2000. In almost all cases, financial information applies to the year 1997–98.

SURVEY RESULTS

1. If the schools responding to the surveys in this report are representative it suggests, as an indicative estimate, that maintained primary and secondary schools and special schools in England may be raising around £230 million a year from sources outside their main school budgets. This is made up of about:
   - £77 million a year in 18,312 primary schools;
   - £143 million a year in 3,567 secondary schools;
   - £11 million a year in 1,229 special schools.

   Allowing for inflation, this is only a small increase on estimates made a decade ago by DSC, NFER and others, which including parental, trust and company contributions were around £130–£140 million a year, equivalent to £180–£200 million in today's money.

2. On the same basis, about 850 independent secondary schools may be raising around £210 million a year, though this estimate is less reliable: 25% of schools surveyed did not give a figure.

3. The amounts raised by maintained schools remain tiny (1%) in comparison with government expenditure on schools in England in 1997–98: £6.7 billion on primary schools; £8.37 billion on secondary schools; plus a further £2 billion on capital expenditure and other items – in all, a total of around £17 billion.

4. In 1997–98, 61% of primary schools surveyed raised between £1,000 and £5,000 a year; 6% raised over £10,000; 1% raised over £25,000. The spread was wider for surveyed secondary schools: 49% raised over £10,000; 29% raised over £25,000; 3% raised between £250,000 and £500,000.

5. The range for surveyed independent schools was still more striking: 70% raised over £10,000; 58% raised over £25,000; and 39% raised over £250,000. Only 3% of maintained secondary schools raised over £250,000. In the 'over £250,000' independent schools, the average per school was over £500,000 a year. But if the 'over £250,000' schools are excluded from the both of these categories, the average per 'ordinary' independent school is virtually the same (about £31,000 against £30,000) as for the majority of the secondary schools.

6. 20% of primary schools and 5% of secondary schools were raising less than £1,000 a year from all sources. Schools in deprived areas, that could not call on parental funding support, were doubly disadvantaged by their difficulties in raising other types of supplementary funding:
   - 56% of primary schools with over 50% of pupils receiving free school meals raised under £1,000; whereas
   - only 10% of those with less than 10% on free school meals raised under £1,000;
   - 47% of secondary schools with over half on free school meals raised under £5,000; whereas
   - only 25% of those with less than 10% on free school meals raised under £5,000.

7. Factors in fundraising success, apart from location in advantaged areas, include parental, company and trust involvement, and knowledge of how to make effective bid and grant applications. Company and trust support of the primary sector (though not the secondary sector) appears to be skewed towards the 'advantaged' schools. Charitable trusts were still significant supporters of independent schools. Disadvantaged schools were heavily dependent on governmental funding such as SRB and GEST/Standards Fund.

8 For the typical school, fundraising methods were still heavily concentrated on 'events'. High fundraising schools, and independent and secondary schools especially, tended also to use more sophisticated fundraising methods, such as trading, commercial sponsorship and covenanting.

- 56% of independent schools and 24% of secondary schools used covenants, compared with only 3% of primary schools.
- 32% of independent schools had long-term development appeals, as did 21% of secondary schools and 16% of special schools. Only 9% of primary schools had development appeals. Voluntary aided schools had a tradition of fundraising. Girls' schools found the going harder.

9 Funds were raised for a wide range of purposes, especially computers, music and sports equipment, and books or library, but very seldom to cover staff salary costs.

10 Many schools, including most primary schools, commented on the disproportionate amount of headteachers' time involved in all forms of fundraising and on the lack of information and the difficulties of bidding for government funds and applying for trust, company, National Lottery and similar grants.

11 A remarkable performance was reported by schools in raising money themselves for other charitable and community causes. If the survey schools were representative, then the total amount raised for charities and local community causes by maintained primary and secondary schools and special schools in England in 1997–98 was £30 million, made up as follows: maintained primary schools – £15 million a year or 19% of what they raised for themselves; maintained secondary schools – £14 million a year, or 10% of what they raised for themselves; special schools – £0.5 million a year or 5% of what they raised for themselves, a prime example of children in need helping to raise funds for other needy children.

12 On the same basis, independent secondary schools were raising £6 million a year for charity and community causes, or 3% of what they raised for themselves (although the amounts per school were the highest in the survey).

CONCLUSIONS AND RECOMMENDATIONS

1 The old assumption that charitable funds should not substitute for public funding is frayed at the edges. The key question, 'What should be provided from public funds and what is it acceptable for a school to raise money for externally?' remains under-defined. There is neither public consensus nor political leadership on this central question, and most maintained schools remain reluctant fundraisers, differing from most charity fundraisers in their uncertainty about whether or not it is right to seek funds from the public, and if so, for what. This issue needs public debate and policy guidance from government.

2 School fundraising should not detract from the obligation on government to fund schools with a level of direct core funding sufficient to deliver the government's own targets, taking account of disadvantage and individual schools' circumstances. The government should consider establishing the definition of a 'Hallmark' school (akin to a British Standard), defining the minimum level of premises, equipment, staffing etc. required to meet the varying needs of pupils. This would provide a means, to match existing measures of schools that 'underperform' in terms of achievement, and to identify those that are 'underprovided' in terms of basic provision, and act as a guide for both statutory and voluntary funders.

3 'Extra-curricular' fundraising should be just that: not an assumed component of maintained schools' budgets, but raising support for items and projects that lie outside that which must be adequately resourced by central and local government.

4 Many charitable trusts have opted wholly or largely out of this difficult area, on the grounds of not substituting for statutory funding; but they remain key funders of the independent sector, tending to reinforce the inequity already inherent in the situation. Companies generally seek to distribute their support more equitably, but usually direct their benefit primarily towards the areas in which they are situated.

Trusts and companies should review their policies to ensure that their input, especially where tax-relieved, contributes to the achievement of equality of opportunity and raising the standards of lower achieving schools within their areas of benefit, and/or of supporting genuine innovation in school – community and extra-curricular projects.

5 The establishment of new Education Trusts (able to hold funds collected from the public and communit, and to use them, at the discretion of a trustee board for defined educational purposes) would benefit all schools. This would give companies, charitable trusts and the general public a means, currently unavailable, of contributing to the advancement of education without committing this support to an individual school. Trusts could be set up on an area basis or to meet specific objectives such as educational research or school library development.

6 Particular attention should be paid to the need of special schools, especially those whose pupils' special needs are compounded by social deprivation.

7 School fundraising is a major and probably disproportionate distraction, in both time and effort, from the principal roles of teachers, and headteachers in particular. Many independent schools can afford professional help; maintained schools usually cannot. Help and resourcing for appropriate school fundraising should be recognised as a training and support need.

8 Fundraising is often associated with activities intended to foster links between schools, parents and the wider community, including local employers. Many schools would gain by refocusing their efforts to raise the standards of their schools and pupils by developing a wider range of methods for involving parents and other stakeholders, and by valuing donated time at least as highly as cash. Senior teachers might benefit from training in how best to manage and motivate volunteers.

9 The accountability, regulation and transparency of charitable funds in schools remains a mess. The DfEE, the Charity Commission and the Local Education Authorities have not given the necessary lead to identify and spread proper and easily managed audit and accountability procedures for school voluntary funds. They should do this and ensure that all schools have equal access to information on how to tap charitable and other sources of supplementary funding.

10 Most school funds and associated charities are now exempt from regulation by the Charity Commission, returning to the historical view that the DfEE can adequately supervise them. In practice this is a big gap in the system; DfEE and the Charity Commission should work together to establish a means (e.g. a 'Schools House', akin to Companies House) to make available and to inspect accounts showing the full extent, sources and use of school voluntary income.

11 The tax benefits available to all schools, and the charitable independent schools in particular, should be re-examined in the light of the national priority to advance education for socially excluded or disadvantaged pupils. Tax relief for parental covenants to school support associations is inconsistent with the prohibition on charitable giving for private benefit.

INTRODUCTION

This report, supported by the Baring Foundation, follows from earlier Directory of Social Change (DSC) policy reports, directories, conferences and training seminars for teachers and governors, which have tracked the extent and impact of school fundraising, the charitable funding of education, and the changing relationship between schools and charity over the last decade.

The purpose of the report is to update and reassess DSC's earlier work in the light of the general perception that schools are needing more and more to look to voluntary sources to supplement their income. We wanted to test anecdotal evidence from parents, teachers and governors against more statistically significant data than had previously been available to us. And we wanted to ascertain what shifts of opinion, if any, had occurred in the context of a new Labour government. Our objective has been not merely to quantify the overall amount raised by schools, which remains a relatively small sum, but to explore the broad pattern of school fundraising, and the attitudes and motivations behind fundraising schools.

The response to our postal survey exceeded our expectations. Not only did more than 1,000 headteachers complete the 8-page questionnaire, many also attached detailed written comments. These reflected a widespread concern about fairness in funding, access to up-to-date information, time pressures, general cost-effectiveness and unclear accountability requirements.

BACKGROUND TO THE SURVEY

In the late 1980s, schools sought for the first time to balance and supplement their newly delegated school budgets. School fundraising, a long familiar but low-key feature of school life, underwent a change of character. The old consensus had been that additional funds should be raised only for 'extras' lying outside the basic curriculum: it was the statutory duty of government and the tax-payer to provide, in the words of the 1944 Education Act, schools sufficient in 'number, character and equipment to afford for all pupils opportunities for education offering such variety of instruction as may be desirable in view of their different ages, abilities and aptitudes...'. It seemed in the late 1980s as if this consensus had disappeared, or was beginning to do so.

The development of 'diversity'

The 1988 Education Reform Act was notable for the major changes it made to the structure and funding of schools. These reflected the Conservative government's wish to introduce greater choice and diversity into the education system, and in particular to encourage greater freedom from local authority control and greater involvement by business. Influential new measures introduced by the Act included:

- Local Management of Schools (LMS)
- The National Curriculum
- Grant maintained Schools (GM)
- City Technology Colleges (CTC)

The Act raised a number of important issues relevant to charity fundraising and management. It created two new types of school with charitable status, soon shortened to GM schools and CTCs. It encouraged businesses to invest more actively in schools. And it unleashed a wave of school fundraising of a scale, in ambition at least, hitherto unknown.

The increased pressure on schools to fundraise

The National Curriculum was presented as an 'entitlement', but with one essential missing component: the money to re-equip the schools, including bringing many long-neglected buildings and classrooms up to standard. Alongside the pressure to fit schools to deliver the National Curriculum came the IT revolution and an associated demand for more and better school computer hardware and software. How much would all this cost? And whose task was it to finance the changes?

Schools seeking to meet the new demands through fundraising found themselves caught in a perpetual treadmill if they were to keep the new computers in good repair and, as necessary, to replace or upgrade. Many school governing bodies were shocked into action by a close examination of how their schools were, or were not, equipped and staffed. At the same time, as the new LMS formula-funded budgets began to bite, a few schools embarked on widely publicised but generally short-lived efforts to raise enough voluntary funding to employ staff who might otherwise face redundancy.

A change of ethos

In a political climate that stressed entrepreneurship and individualism, a notable shift in ethos took place. Maintained sector schools suddenly began to see themselves in competition with others for pupils and for funds. The big change was not so much that schools were raising money for essential core equipment: many had long done so, if surreptitiously. It was that they felt expected and indeed encouraged to do so. Self-help was back.

Business in the school community

Until the late 1980s, schools wishing to fundraise had looked largely to parents for extra resources. Even the voluntary aided schools, whose diocesan bodies or founding trusts were statutorily required to contribute 15% of their capital buildings and external maintenance costs, often called on parental help when setting up fundraising appeals for new buildings. Although in many places pioneering School–Industry projects and early Education Business Partnerships were creating valuable new links between schools and the world outside, it was still relatively unusual for a school to seek major funding from the business sector. After 1988, some school fundraising plans became wide-ranging and ambitious. In at least one area schools were actively encouraged by their LEA to generate additional income from hitherto unconsidered sources, such as letting their premises, offering services to local companies, displaying advertisements in school corridors and company logos on exercise books.

The growth of the fundraising PTA charities

Before 1988, some headteachers still refused to let parents hold meetings on school premises. The early Parent–Teacher Associations (PTAs) were set up to benefit the pupils by encouraging better communication between the school and the parents. PTA fundraising was a secondary matter and usually on a modest scale, such as organising the annual summer fair or a school disco. The idea that the management committee of a PTA might also be its charity trustees was far from most minds. Since at the time small charities in England and Wales were only required to register if they possessed annual 'investment income' of £15 or more, the matter was scarcely pressing. Few PTAs received interest of any kind on their modest bank accounts.

In the late 1980s, the Department of Education and Science helped fund a leaflet distributed by the National Confederation of Parent–Teacher Associations (NCPTA) drawing to the attention of maintained sector schools the tax benefits available to those, particularly in the corporate sector, who donated money or gifts in kind to a school for educational purposes. As registered educational charities, PTAs and Friends' Associations could accept charitable donations on behalf of a school, whether or not the school was entitled in its own right to claim the tax benefits of charitable status. The NCPTA standard constitution for its members was approved by the Charity Commission as suitable for a charity. And in the years that followed, the numbers of PTAs (also known as HSAs, or Home–School Associations) and school Friends' Associations that sought registration as charities hugely increased.

The independent sector

Through the 1980s the position of the public schools (rebranded a decade earlier as part of the 'independent sector') remained secure. In the months before the 1992 election, many independent schools feared the loss of their charitable status and campaigned vigorously for retention of independence and, in schools constituted as charities, for the tax and other advantages that flowed from charitable status. Today neither of the main political parties appears to have any appetite for tackling the old public schools debate; nor are there any major threats to the tax status of the independent sector. Many of the tax benefits of charitable status are now available to community (county) schools with registered PTAs. Despite this, the greatest tax advantages continue to go to the very small number of independent schools with extensive property holdings and high levels of investment income.

However, the government has begun to press independent schools to share their specialist facilities, often in language teaching, sports and arts, with local maintained schools. Another change that may lie ahead is the greater willingness of the present government to consider applications from independent schools that would prefer to become part of the maintained sector.

New century, new realism?

Twelve years on from the Education Reform Act 1988, it is certainly true that schools are still more active fundraisers than was once the case. But as the present survey shows, there is now a new sense of realism, in some cases of disillusion, about what can be achieved. The expectation that headteachers can generate additional income from their local community for a variety of purposes, including match-funding, has become a source of stress. A few enthusiastic entrepreneurs enjoy the competitive race for funding; far more are reluctant but duty-bound, and many are disheartened by their time-consuming failure to tap funds that they believed were 'out there'.

City Academies

As this report was going to press, the government announced its plans for the creation of City Academies. Although presented as a radical new step, this is in many ways reminiscent of the previous government's efforts to break up local authority control of education and to introduce greater diversity and choice into the comprehensive system by setting up GM schools and CTCs. Unlike the Education Action Zones, where several schools, sometimes more than a dozen, were grouped together, a City Academy will be an individual school set up to offer a new start for a 'failing school', either by replacing it or by taking it over. The Academies will be publicly funded but run in partnership with government by a mixture of voluntary, parent, teacher and for-profit private companies.

What part the voluntary sector and trust and company donors (as against private for-profit companies) will play in this revolution remains to be seen. In America, which has over fifteen years' experience of similar efforts to introduce competition into public education, opinion remains divided.

No matter what the outcome, the question of equality of opportunity remains and must not be forgotten. In their influential book *Reinventing Government*, the American writers Osborne and Gaebler quote approvingly the views of a leader of the Minnesota school reform, Verne Johnson. They serve as a useful warning and guideline:

'Public policy absolutely must control what kind of competition takes place, and public policy and financing must take care of those who don't have enough money. Deregulating everything means that the people with money win and the rest of them lose, and we can't have that.'

Does the issue of school fundraising really matter?

Overall, the amounts fundraised by schools remain tiny in comparison with the billions invested in education by government. There are many other factors (including, for example, local authority boundaries and differences in the formulae of school delegated budgets) that can have far greater consequences for an individual school's finances. For these reasons, the fundraising issue may seem very minor, even unimportant.

But at school level, where typically 90% of a school's budget is absorbed by salaries, fundraised voluntary income can make a difference, not least to equality of opportunity. Some maintained schools raise very little or nothing at all; a few others raise very large amounts indeed. This hidden financial fault line is running through the maintained sector and widening, unobserved. What effect will it have? Of course standards do not depend solely on budgets. But it would be foolish to pretend that money plays no part in determining what a school has to offer or what its pupils can achieve.

CHARITABLE STATUS: A TANGLED WEB

Legislation from the 1988 Education Reform Act onwards has extended the charitable status of schools and their associated fundraising instruments. But the legal implications, and their consequences for the personal liability of school governors and others holding school voluntary funds, remain opaque. The following paragraphs try to untangle this knotty subject but conclude that it needs government action to cut through the undergrowth and point the way ahead.

Until 1988, it was only the independent schools and the voluntary schools for whom the advantages and obligations of school charitable status were relevant. Within the state sector, voluntary schools in England and Wales were 'excepted' from the duty to register with the Charity Commission where their governing bodies controlled no assets other than the school premises. They remained under the jurisdiction of the Charity Commission, which had the right, seldom exercised, to call in their accounts.

The Education Reform Act 1988

Under the 1988 Education Reform Act, voluntary schools retained their status as excepted charities because they were under the trusteeship and supervision of non-statutory charitable bodies, usually the churches. The county schools, which were established and owned by local authorities, were not charities but activities of statutory bodies, and this situation was not changed by the 1988 Act. The new GM schools, however, were declared in the Act to be 'exempt' charities; this meant that, as well as not having to register with the Charity Commission, they lay outside its jurisdiction altogether (though still bound by charity law).

Grant maintained schools were, by any other definition, very odd charities indeed. Since all their funding came from a government agency, the Secretary of State for Education retained considerable influence over their governing bodies, and their freedom to select their own beneficiaries was limited by statute. But because statute, which trumps all, said they were exempt charities, they were. Until this time, exempt charitable status had been a privilege extended to only two schools: Eton and Winchester, though it also applied to many universities.

As well as declaring the grant maintained schools exempt charities, the Education Reform Act 1988 made subsidiary organisations and trust funds connected with these schools also exempt. This covered, for example, appeal funds and prize funds under the same or very similar trusteeship as the governing body. It did not cover independently established parent–teacher or other school support associations. PTAs of grant maintained schools, like others, were required to register with the Charity Commission if they conformed to the legal definition of a charity and passed its assets threshold. The new City Technology Colleges created by the Act were not exempted, but took the form of charitable companies limited by guarantee. Although established by statute, and non-fee paying, CTCs were registered as independent schools and today are notably and curiously excluded from DfEE maintained school statistics.

The post-1988 situation raised many questions for those interested in the legal position it created. If state schools were to become more active players, even if indirectly, in the fundraising pool, to whom were schools accountable for their use of what many headteachers called their 'voluntary' or 'private' funds? Who were the trustees of these non-statutory school funds? Were School Funds required to register with the Charity Commision? And if not who would, at least in theory, act as a regulatory body?

The Charities Act 1992

The 1992 Charities Act brought the activities of small charities under tighter supervision. Charities in England and Wales were now required to register with the Charity Commission once they had annual income (not 'investment income', as in the 1960 Charities Act) of more than £1,000. If a charity's annual income exceeded £10,000, it became additionally required to submit its annual accounts to the Charity Commission (in England and Wales) and to the Inland Revenue (for charities in other parts of the UK).

But what about the GM schools that had recently, perhaps without much thought, been made 'exempt charities'? Their governors were now charity trustees, even if exempt from the duty to register: what would be their personal liabilities if things went wrong? No-one was quite sure, and in truth, very few were seriously at risk. But the risk was there: although the 1988 Education Reform Act had incorporated the governing bodies of grant maintained schools, this did not, in the view of many charity lawyers, lessen personal liability to the degree that the incorporation of the schools' trust funds themselves might have done.

The Education Act 1993

The Education Act 1993 made all school governing bodies into bodies corporate, though the implications of this with regard to the trusteeship of school voluntary/charitable funds were still far from clear. In the House of Lords in May 1993, speaking for the government on a probing amendment during the debates that led to the Act, Lord Henley conceded that at least some of the 'gifts of money, land and other property' held or applied by school governing bodies for the advancement of education were likely to be held on charitable trust. The amendment was withdrawn when he indicated that published guidance might emerge as a result of his statement. A new government has come, the House of Lords as it was then has gone, and no guidance has been published.

The School Standards and Framework Act 1998

When the new Labour government was elected in 1997, some thought there might be more radical changes to the school structure than was actually the case. The charitable status of the independent sector remains intact, though the assisted places scheme was withdrawn. Recent discussion between the charitable independent schools and government has been based on how best to make some of their facilities, such as specialist subject teaching and sports facilities available to local maintained schools.

As for the GM schools, the expectation had been that their separate status might end, and that they would return to their previous county school or voluntary school status. Instead some complicated adjustments to 'the framework' took place.

Under the School Standards and Framework Act 1998 all maintained schools became either:

- community schools (previously 'county' schools)
- foundation schools (the category adopted by most of those previously grant maintained)
- voluntary schools, still of two types, aided and controlled (with some grant maintained schools returning to aided status)
- community special schools
- foundation special schools.

The governing bodies of all existing and new foundation schools became exempt charities for the purposes of the Charities Act 1993. So, for the first time, did the governing bodies of voluntary schools. However 'no governing body of a community or community special school' was to be a charity.

Charitable status of PTAs, School Funds, etc.

Where did this leave the unanswered matter of the status of school funds held by governing bodies? The 1988 Education Reform Act, in the case of the grant maintained schools, had made not only the schools themselves but also 'institutions connected with' them exempt charities. Similar provisions were carried through into the 1998 Standards and Framework Act for foundation and voluntary schools, so 'institutions established for the purposes of the school, or in connection with it' were confirmed as having exempt charitable status. In practice, this meant that any subsidiary school charities or charitable funds attached to foundation and voluntary schools in England and Wales would not need to register with the Charity Commission but could, as do charities in Scotland, claim recognition by and charitable tax reliefs directly from the Inland Revenue.

The Charity Commission currently explains the position as follows:

• for community schools in England and Wales, a PTA or Friends' Association constituted as a charity will be required to register if its assets pass the income threshold (now set at more than £1,000 a year – in gross income, not interest). Once charitable income passes the £10,000 threshold, the charity will be required to submit an annual report and accounts, in the usual manner.

• a School Fund holding voluntary income will be required to register if it passes the threshold. (No guidance is given on the fact that the governing body itself, which holds the fund, is explicitly declared in the Act not to be a charity. Presumably the implication is that a community school holding voluntary funds for the advancement of education would, once these assets passed the threshold, be expected to establish a separate trust for such assets. Yet the Act still places 'gifts and donations' to a school under the trusteeship of the governing body, itself explicitly 'not a charity'.)

• in foundation and voluntary schools in England and Wales, the Commission says that PTAs, if constituted as charities, are required to register and submit accounts on the same basis as those of community schools. (However, in view of the wording of Section 23 of the Act, which allows exemption to any institution established 'for the general purposes of, or for any special purpose of or in connections with [an exempt school]' this is open to question, particularly where governors set up or form the majority amongst the office holders of a foundation school's PTA or Friends' Association.)

• school trustees (i.e. the founding bodies of voluntary schools) are required to register only if they hold assets other than the school premises; the governing bodies of the schools themselves and any voluntary funds they hold are exempt.

This makes little sense, except to legal logic. It surely calls for a simpler system, where accounts of all voluntary school funds and PTA/support organisations are either deregulated (with the ensuing risk of negligence or fraud) or else all answerable to the same body and required to meet the same standards of good practice.

Who regulates?

Where in all this is accountability? What would happen if something went wrong within an exempt school charity, for example if the appeal committee of a foundation school entered into contracts and commitments it could not meet, or if trustees of a development fund were concerned about possible fraud? Since the schools and some, at least, of their 'connected institutions' are exempt from Charity Commission registration and supervision, who has the duty of overseeing them? Any inquiry into breaches of their trusts would have to be brought by the Attorney-General in the High Courts. At some point, the Secretary of State may well be called to launch an inquiry requiring knowledge of charity law outside the expertise of the DfEE.

School governors and HSAs/PTAs, particularly in foundation and voluntary aided schools, deserve more authoritative guidance than is at present available to them about the nature of trusteeship, their obligations and their protection in this area.

The central questions

The old debates of the 1970s and early 1990s on the charitable status of the public schools have to some extent been overtaken. Today maintained and independent not-for-profit schools have access to very similar tax benefits, although not on an identical basis, not always through the same mechanisms and, in the case of the leading public schools with high investment income, by no means with the same outcomes.

The newer challenge is to ask with an open mind how freedom, choice, innovation and diversity can best be combined with equity; how to reduce 'unfair' competition for educational and life opportunities; whether senior teachers' time is being best spent completing bid and grant applications; what contribution, if any, school fundraising could make to the national endeavour to provide equality of opportunity and high standards for all children; and what part underprovision may play in underachievement.

THE SURVEY: AIMS AND METHODOLOGY

This report draws on surveys carried out by the Directory of Social Change in 1999, when primary and secondary maintained schools, special and independent schools in England were surveyed. The schools were assured of their anonymity.

The researchers' aims were to investigate the extent, uses and sources of school funds raised from all non-LEA sources by schools in England, how these funds were managed and how headteachers viewed what seemed to be their growing responsibility for generating additional forms of income for their schools.

The main areas we wanted to explore were:
- how much is raised by schools in England
- what schools raise money for
- how schools raise money
- what are their main sources of support
- the impact of the National Lottery
- factors affecting school fundraising
- fundraising, deprivation and disadvantage
- who organises the fundraising and holds the funds
- the difficulties schools encounter and their information needs
- how much schools raise for non-school charities

We also looked separately, in supplementary surveys, at:
- the experience of independent secondary schools
- the experience of special schools

Methodology

Details of the number of schools mailed and the response rates are shown in each of the *Survey Findings* sections. The surveys differed slightly: the primary survey was directed to all schools in four areas; the secondary schools were a representative sample selected from throughout England.

THE SURVEY: OVERVIEW OF FINDINGS

Responses

Whilst we were pleased with the high response rates (c.25%), we were also aware of the 'Sherlock Holmes factor': the dogs that had not barked in the night. There was at least some possibility that a number of the non-responding schools were exceptionally high fundraisers, unwilling, even under conditions of assured anonymity, to disclose the amounts raised, their fundraising techniques or carefully cultivated sources of support. Such schools might fear that if central or local government were to learn how much they raise through their own efforts, the result could be a cutback in their statutory funding. Conversely, less fortunate schools failing to respond may have had little or nothing on which to report, or may have actively disapproved of fundraising. Many are likely to share the fear of their more fortunate colleagues, that publicity on this issue could encourage government to expect fundraising to play a part in the income generation of all schools.

Amounts raised

We did not ask schools the precise amounts they raised, but into which of a number of bands their total fell. Even on the assumption that the responding schools were representative of all English schools, this did not give a total figure for amounts raised. In order to make an indicative estimate, we made the further assumption that each school (on average) lay at the mid-point of the band they said they belonged to; thus a school saying that they raised between £1,000 and £5,000 was scored as raising £3,000 for this purpose. On this basis we made an indicative estimate for all English maintained primary and secondary schools of just over £230 million. This is made up of: primary – £77 million; secondary – £210 million; Special – £11 million.

The true amount could, of course, lie quite a long way either side of this figure. Especially in the case of secondary schools, the results are heavily influenced by a relatively small number of very high fundraisers, and this could skew the indicative estimate by a considerable amount. (The same is even more true of the indicative estimate we separately made of the independent schools – £210 million. Nevertheless, the method we used allows some comparison to be made between the independent and maintained sectors.)

How does this compare?

If the figure of just over £230 million for all maintained schools in England is of the right order, how does this compare with the situation a decade ago? In 1990, a survey conducted for the Mail on Sunday by the National Foundation for Education Research, just before the introduction of local management of schools, suggested that primary schools alone were raising funds of around £40 million a year from parents, companies and trusts combined. In *State Schools – A Suitable Case For Charity?* [Mountfield, DSC 1991] fundraising in all UK maintained schools was estimated to be in the region of £130–£140 million in terms of cash and gifts in kind, or considerably more, up to £230 million, if the cost of staff time in companies supporting education in various ways were taken into account. (£130–£140 million in 1989 is equivalent to £180–£200 million today.) The present research applies only to schools in England, and so is not directly comparable. Nevertheless, after allowing for inflation of about 40% in total between 1989 and 1998, the total estimated in this report is not vastly greater than a decade ago.

We do not yet see all maintained schools earning money for core costs by advertising in their corridors, stationery and roof tops, getting commission on insurance for parents or running for-profit after-school care centres, boarding units and weekend-only car parks (though all of these have been tried by a school somewhere). Nor are all parents, although certain high-placed ones are, being invited to subscribe termly to their children's schools. Most schools have abandoned the effort to raise funds for teachers' salaries. It is, however, commonplace to raise money for school books, IT equipment and buildings on a scale that would have been unthinkable 20 years ago.

For those who see the funding of maintained schools as a prime responsibility of government, this conclusion, if correct, is a moderately heartening one, so far as it goes.

SOURCES OF FUNDS

Parents and friends

The vast majority of schools said that Home–School or Parent–Teacher Associations, or Friends' Associations were their main source of non-LEA funding. But the contribution parents can make is clearly influenced by their own prosperity: schools with high proportions of pupils receiving free school meals (which we used as a convenient, if imperfect, indicator of disadvantage) raised significantly less in total than schools where few pupils received free school meals.

The bid culture, companies and charitable trusts

Increasingly, state education is an arena for partnership funding and complex bidding procedures to non-educational official funders and agencies as well as educational sources.

Many schools, especially those raising the higher amounts, made use of many sources of funding and gifts, including Education Business Partnerships, TECs, SRB and a wide range of other official funds, and charitable trusts. Several schools commented on the complexity and difficulty of the applications, business plans, costings and so on that were required, not only for the various government and local authority sources of funds but also by companies and trusts.

In the case of primary schools, company and trust funding went much more to the haves than to the have-nots; interestingly this was not the case with secondary schools, where the companies and trusts helped similar proportions of advantaged and disadvantaged schools (though we have no evidence of the amounts in each case).

Charitable trusts were still seen as major supporters of the independent sector.

The National Lottery and the New Opportunities Fund

Very few schools had so far benefited from the National Lottery (since the original rules greatly limited the extent to which publicly-funded educational bodies could benefit). The New Opportunities Fund, however, did open up a new source. When the questionnaires were sent out, the New Opportunities Fund had just begun to register in school fundraising. At least half of all maintained schools were intending to apply to the fund; some were not looking to apply; a good number were undecided, and a significant proportion did not feel they had sufficient information to make a judgement. As the fund was in its very early stages when the research was conducted, this may not be surprising. However, there are important questions raised by the lack of funding information generally, and about how information is disseminated and shared. With a development as potentially important as the New Opportunities Fund to the funding of education, it is fundamental to ensure that all schools receive the same information at the same time.

Development appeals

A relatively small number of maintained schools had formal development appeals, for a wide range of specified purposes. These were usually held separately from the school's other fundraised income, since they tended to be for long-term projects.

How funds are managed and held within the school

Where the PTA was the main non-LEA contributor, the person with main responsibility for organising fundraising in the school was more often than not the headteacher or a senior management team member. A number of schools were reluctant to choose one person or group as having the main responsibility, with some naming the headteacher, deputy head, department head, parents and development officer. Unlike the independent sector, only a minority of maintained schools appeared to have a development officer, a resources manager or an external fundraiser.

Schools commented, for example, that their Friends' Association was the same thing as their HSA or PTA. There appeared to be much higher awareness of charity registration requirements amongst the support associations than within the schools.

Pressure on teachers

We have allowed the voice of the teachers, mostly headteachers, to be heard because their concerns are both values-led and practical. Fundraising is occupying more time than perhaps it deserves, and adding new pressures to already over-burdened professionals. We have called throughout this report for government to make its vision for the future of fair funding of schools explicit. The teaching unions and others, including Ofsted, should also make their views known, and in particular seek to ensure that all schools have equal access to the guidance, information and training necessary for appropriate and successful fundraising.

Fundraising for others: charities and community causes

Charities view schools as a source of income and some engage in marketing their cause vigorously to schools. As many headteachers were meeting increasing demands to fundraise for the school itself, it was important to find out where charity fundraising fitted in to the school's priorities. The survey shows a remarkable commitment to supporting constituencies other than the school. The results suggest that in total, maintained primary and secondary schools raise nearly £30 million a year for charitable and community causes, despite the pressing needs of the schools themselves.

There were warning signs that there may be a limit to the effort schools are prepared to put into non-school fundraising, particularly where their own voluntary funds may suffer as a result. One school reported 'We are looking seriously at how much money can be raised in future as a result of severe financial cuts the school has recently undergone'. Another said 'Increasingly we feel we need to direct pupil energy towards school necessities'.

Charities would do well to consider their approach to schools. There are clear indications from the survey that many schools feel that there are now too many requests from charities competing for the limited resources that schools can offer. One school commented, 'Charities seem to think that schools are bottomless pits of money that they can continually ask to raise money'. Although it was felt that it was getting harder to raise money, there was a balancing impression that it was still easier to raise money for an outside charity than for the school itself. Educational and personal development opportunities offered by charities were looked at very favourably by schools when sifting the large number of requests that they received.

There are good foundations for charities to build upon when approaching schools. The more a charity can relate its information to the school curriculum or to pupils' own interests, and the more it can centre its school campaigns on events and activities that engage the interests of pupils and teachers, the better the experience will be for both sides.

How the rest of the report is organised

The next sections deal separately with the main survey results for primary and secondary schools, followed by shorter and less detailed supplementary surveys of special and independent schools. We have adopted similar numbered headings throughout all four sections, to make it easier to cross refer. This approach also necessitated a degree of repetition, in the interests of presenting self-contained sections on each sector.

The Findings are followed by a selection of comments from headteachers in all types of school surveyed.

Finally, there is a section containing *Policy Conclusions and Recommendations*.

FINDINGS

FUNDRAISING IN PRIMARY SCHOOLS IN ENGLAND

This survey of 492 maintained primary schools in England was carried out in October–December 1999.

MAIN FINDINGS

How much primary schools raise

Of the primary schools responding:
- 20% were raising less than £1,000 a year, or nothing at all;
- 6% were raising £10,000 or more a year;
  of these:
  1% were raising £25,000 or more a year;
  2 schools surveyed were raising more than £50,000–£100,000 a year;
- most primary schools (61%) were raising between £1,000–£5,000 a year.
- the spread of funds was generally less than that indicated in the secondary schools survey.

An indicative estimate of the amounts raised by all primary schools in England can be made on the basis of these figures. Schools were not asked to display the precise amount raised, but to say into which of a number of bands their fundraising fell. On the assumption that the responding schools were representative, and that, on average, their fundraised income lay at the middle of the band named, national figures as follows are indicated for maintained primary schools in England:

- £77 million a year raised by maintained English primary schools from sources outside their main school budget;
- just over £4,200 a year on average per school (i.e. approximately £18 per pupil), although the spread around these numbers may be considerable.

Main sources of support for primary schools

- at least for the great majority of schools, parents continue to be the first call for primary school fundraising, although they are not necessarily the biggest single source in high fundraising schools;
- companies, charitable trusts and diocesan bodies were the highest non-governmental/LEA and non-parental funders of primary schools, though not on the same scale as in secondary schools;
- where the percentage of pupils receiving free school meals is the measure of disadvantage, companies and trusts showed a strong bias towards the more 'advantaged' school, (i.e. those where fewer than 10% of pupils receive free meals).
- SRB, GEST/Standards Fund and similar forms of bid funding were often the only sources of additional income to benefit primary schools in poor areas;
- 47% of maintained primary schools surveyed were intending to apply to the New Opportunities Fund.

Factors affecting primary school fundraising include:

- the availability to the schools of up-to-date information about funding opportunities and the time and expertise required to raise significant sums from specialist bids, including European and Challenge/SRB funding, charitable trusts, company donors and sponsors;

- the involvement of parents and others in the wider community, and their ability to provide financial support (noting that the first does not necessarily imply the second);
- primary schools were more heavily dependent on parental support than other types of school, and the amounts they raised were therefore likely to reflect the home circumstances of the pupils;
- the presence, or not, of various types of external funding bodies (government funds and agencies, companies, trusts etc.) willing to provide financial help, gifts in kind and advice. These have particular impact in areas where primary school parents cannot provide financial support;
- the relevance of area: despite the varying levels of economic activity in each primary school area surveyed, fundraising approaches and results varied less than expected between the 'rural' and the 'urban' areas. The chief relevance of area is likely to be the presence, or not, of parents with disposable income and the presence, or not, of various types of external funding bodies, including donor companies;
- 79% of English primary schools responding said they needed more information and training on sources and methods of fundraising;
- 37% of English primary schools responding said they had insufficient information about the New Opportunities Fund.

Primary school fundraising for charitable and community causes

Of the primary schools responding:
- 89% said they raised money for charities and community causes.
- an average of £801 a year was being raised by all maintained primary schools surveyed. We counted the non-responding schools as raising zero income for others.

An indicative national estimate, if these samples are assumed to be representative, is that:

- primary schools in England may be raising almost £15 million a year for charities and local community causes: 19% of the amount they raise for themselves.

HOW THE RESEARCH WAS CARRIED OUT

This survey into school fundraising in primary schools in England was carried out in 1999–2000. In almost all cases the financial information it contains applies to the year 1997–98.

Sample

In October 1999 questionnaires were sent to 2,007 schools, i.e. about 11% of all 18,312 primary schools in England. This mailing, unlike the secondary survey, was not evenly distributed across the whole country; instead it went to all primary schools in four pre-selected areas.

Area A/r was in the south of England; Area B/r in the east; Area C/u in the west; Area D/u in the north; as the second letter of their coding indicates, two were primarily urban and two primarily rural areas. Community, foundation and voluntary schools were all represented in the sample. The findings below apply only to maintained primary schools. Special schools, many of which are all-age, are separately surveyed.

Response rate

We received 492 replies from the maintained primary schools, a response rate of about 25%, with the lowest reponse rate (22%) coming from the the largest of the four areas (Area D/u). Together the two urban areas represented 65% of the schools mailed, but only 51% of those that responded. Most of the schools responding (76%) had fewer than 300 pupils. Only one response came from a single sex (girls') school.

Data

Where figures used in the tables that follow are not based on the total number of responding schools, the figure from which the table is derived ('the respondents') is stated. Where figures have been rounded, there may be minor discrepancies between the sum of the constituent parts and the totals as shown. Since the questionnaires went to all primary schools in four areas, but not nationwide, a degree of caution should be exercised before drawing national conclusions from this survey.

RESULTS

1 How much is raised by primary schools

Most maintained primary schools in England are still raising relatively small amounts, typically between £1,000 and £5,000 a year. The survey results shown in Table 1, if representative of all primary schools in England, suggest that the total raised by primary schools is around £77 million (with a small number of primary schools also setting high targets for longer-term development appeals). After taking account of 40% inflation between 1989–98, the amounts raised overall were only about a third higher than those estimated ten years ago. 19 primary schools failed to answer the question: 'How much do you raise each year?', possibly for some of the reasons explored earlier in the *Overview of the Findings* (see p16).

TABLE 1
Financial support raised by primary schools, in addition to the main school budget 1997–98.
Respondents: 473

	No. of primary schools	%
Less than £1,000	93	20
£1,001–£5,000	288	61
£5,001–£10,000	64	14
£10,001–£15,000	17	4
£15,001–£25,000	6	1
£25,001–£35,000	1	0.2
£35,001–£50,000	2	0.4
£50,001–£100,000	2	0.4

2 What primary schools raise money for

Table 2 shows the fundraising priorities of responding schools. Hard-won experience of what is and what is not sustainable and attractive to funders is demonstrated by the low positions of two items: teacher salaries (0.6%) – the focus of many desperate and usually unsuccessful fundraising projects ten years ago – and 'stationery' (5%), long regarded by national parent associations and others as the most basic of basics, for which no school should feel obliged to raise supplementary income. The low place of traditional fundraising extras, such as swimming pools and minibuses, was also striking; this is possibly because the maintenance costs have become too high for primary schools, or because other needs were seen as more pressing.

In the order of priority, books (80%), computers (77%), money to pay for school trips (59%) and playground improvements (57%) scored highly in the primary schools. The fact that school trips came third from top was interesting. Many primary schools are now unwilling to organise educational school trips unless all pupils are able to participate. They are not allowed to charge for such visits but often draw on their school voluntary funds for this purpose, to augment their delegated budgets.

TABLE 2.1
What primary schools raise money for

Items	Primary schools naming	% total sample (492)
Books	394	80
Computers	377	77
School trips	288	59
Playground	281	57
Sports equipment	244	50
Library	210	43
Music equipment	195	40
School grounds	153	31
Furniture	110	22
Arts: specialist writers/artists etc	99	20
School buildings	93	19
School holidays/tours	59	12
Gym	33	7
Stationery	24	5
Swimming pool	23	5
Minibuses	13	3
Parents facilities	13	3
Teachers' salaries	3	0.6

Other items

We also gave respondents the opportunity to name some of the other items for which funds were being raised. 59 schools took this opportunity and a selection of the items they named is shown in Table 2.2 below. It confirms our general impression that many primary schools still target their fundraising primarily on core needs (other than teachers' salaries). Compared with the secondary schools, relatively few appear to be fundraising for innovative projects. This reluctance may reflect the greater core funding needs of the primary schools. Or it may reflect the wider experience of fundraising methods and staff time available elsewhere. Although the 10% of primary schools surveyed had 'other items' they wanted to add to our list, others reminded us, with appealing frankness, that they had not succeeded in raising money for any of the items we listed, let alone for anything else. They called for a sense of realism about what could be achieved.

TABLE 2.2
'Other' items named by primary schools as fundraising targets.

Items	Primary schools naming
TV/Video/Audio-visual equipment	9
Swimming (tuition/travel)	9
Carpets/curtains	4
Whiteboards/OHPs	4
Cookery items	3
Staging and lighting	3
Out of school clubs	3
Decoration	2
Community facilities	1
Non-teaching staff	1
No additional items or projects	19

3 How primary schools raise money

We asked if any of eight likely approaches to fundraising had been employed. Primary schools still appeared to rely heavily (72%) on events and other conventional fundraising techniques such as the 200 Club draw ('ours is only a 100 Club!') or the car boot sale. Although 25% of primary schools claimed to be actively seeking sponsorship, we soon became aware that this somewhat ambiguous term had more than one meaning for the schools, particularly at primary level. Some teachers assumed it to refer, as we had expected, to 'company sponsorship' of school teams, brochures and vehicles; others took it to refer to a much simpler and more familiar fundraising method, the 'sponsored swim' or 'sponsored walk', where parents and neighbours sponsor individual children. 25% of primary schools were engaged in minor trading activities (for example, through the sale of school t-shirts, Christmas cards and school photos).

Curiously, only one primary school drew to our attention its success with the ubiquitous commercial vouchers available through supermarkets, newspapers, crisps etc. for school books or computers. Several headteachers commented separately on the ease or difficulty with which they administered these schemes: opinions varied, with some at least regarding the vouchers as a painless form of fundraising, whilst others deplored the need for schools to collect in this way. A small number were experimenting with 'affinity' credit cards, though as yet with little evidence of success.

As the lower half of Table 3.1 shows, it was noticeable that fewer primary schools than secondary and independent secondary schools were seeking to benefit from tax-effective fundraising methods such as covenanting and Gift Aid. This may change as the Chancellor's recently announced tax changes make it easier to give small one-off charity donations tax-effectively through Gift Aid and other measures, without needing to persuade supporters to enter into the longer-term commitment of a covenant.

TABLE 3.1
The most frequently reported fundraising methods in primary schools

	No. of schools naming	% total sample (492)
Events	356	72
Sponsorship	125	25
Trading	125	25
200 Clubs	106	22
Affinity cards	10	2
Tax-effective giving		
Gift Aid	21	4
Covenants	17	3
Legacies	11	2

Development appeals

Relatively few primary schools (43 schools: 9% of the sample, compared with about 20% of secondary schools and over 30% of independent schools) said they had established a development appeal. Unsurprisingly many primary school development appeals were in voluntary aided schools, where the founding trust or Diocesan body is required by law to provide 15% of the costs of new building or external buildings maintenance.

Almost without exception these development appeals were for new buildings or for building repair/alteration, although IT suites also featured. We were interested to learn what types of school had development appeals, what targets the schools were setting themselves and how successful their efforts had been. Table 3.2 shows the categories of school involved, the areas in which they were operating, the purposes of their development appeals and how much had already been raised. Since we did not know when each appeal had started, no firm conclusions should be drawn from the amounts raised so far.

Area D/u had fewer schools (6%) than others adopting this approach, although those that did had ambitious targets. This may reflect the wide range of socio-economic backgrounds of schools and families in this inner and outer city area. We noted also the lower than average targets set by primary schools in Area B/r, overall characterised by its caution.

TABLE 3.2

Primary schools with development appeals
By area, category, purpose and amounts raised

	Area A/r	Area B/r	Area C/u	Area D/u
By category:				
Community	8	4	6	6
Foundation	0	3	0	0
Voluntary Aided	0	0	2	6
Voluntary Controlled	0	3	3	2
Total	8	10	11	14
Overall: 9%				
Appeal for:				
New Buildings	7	8	10	8
Buildings Repair	0	2	0	4
IT suite	1	0	1	2
Targets and Results to date:	£	£	£	£
Highest:				
Target	250,000	50,000	250,000	50,000
Result to date	66,000	15,000	66,000	12,000
Lowest:				
Target	6,000	1,000	10,000	200
Result to date	1,000	250	4,000	845

4 How fundraising is managed in primary schools

We have already noted the high dependence of primary schools on parents as fundraisers. We were also interested to know who managed the activity: who was it that the schools saw as 'responsible' for fundraising.

Who organises the work

Headteachers and parents were strongly in the lead, with school governors notably quite a long way down the list. Since they are ultimately responsible for the schools' financial affairs, this absence from a table compiled by headteachers was striking.

In primary schools the 'department heads' are usually the subject specialists with responsibility for curriculum development. Unlike the secondary schools, the primary schools placed department heads above deputy heads as leaders in fundraising. In small primary schools where often the headteachers have a full teaching timetable, the lack of human resource to investigate and write up complicated bids and applications was the focus of regular and forceful comment.

TABLE 4.1

Persons named as having prime responsibility for primary school fundraising

	No. of schools	% total sample (492)
Headteacher	254	52
Parents	253	52
Department head	38	8
Deputy head	28	6
Governors	10	2
Resources manager	2	0.4
Development officer	1	0.2
External fundraiser	1	0.2

The percentages shown in Table 4.1 compare the number of replies with the total sample of responding schools. They do not total 100% because many schools showed more than one person as having 'main responsibility' for fundraising, usually the headteacher and the parents. This is an admirable situation, provided individual responsibilities are clearly defined, in particular who decides how the funds are used. But a frequent complaint from parent fundraisers is that 'We raise it, he spends it'. Or, even more tellingly, 'She puts it in the bank in case one day the roof collapses, so our children never see any benefit whatsoever'.

Development officer, resource manager, fundraiser, fundraising consultant

A very small number of primary schools employed a resource manager, development officer, or fundraising consultant; none seemed to have made a major impact.

Who holds the funds

We also wanted to know who was accountable for the various funds held by schools. Unsurprisingly the 'School Fund' tops the list of contributors, since in almost all schools the School Fund becomes the resting place for monies from sources beyond the statutory; these may include private funds such as money collected towards a school holiday, or charitable donations from an individual or charitable trust.

Table 4.2 indicates the general awareness of charity law within the schools and amongst their supporters. PTA and similar school support organisations seemed remarkably well aware of their obligation to register with the Charity Commission, if they were constituted as independent charities exclusively for the advancement of education, and if their income exceeded the £1,000 annual income threshold. Whether the headteachers and governing bodies who controlled the schools' voluntary income held in a School Fund were as aware of the reporting and accountability requirements for school funds held on trust is more doubtful and, given the present lack of clear guidance, entirely understandable. This issue is discussed at greater length in the *Introduction*.

Again, the percentages in Table 4.2 indicate the proportion of schools naming a particular fund or fund-holder, compared with the total number of schools in the sample; there are overlaps, hence percentages do not total 100. The final right-hand column shows the registered charities in column four as a percentage of the similar funds named in column one. It gives only a rough guide to the general levels of awareness; many charitable PTAs and other organisations hold few or no assets and do not approach the level at which small charity registration becomes a requirement.

TABLE 4.2

Funds contributing to and holding primary school fundraising income

	Fund contributes financially		Fund is a registered charity	
	No. of schools	% total sample	No. of schools	Col. 3 as % col. 1
HSA/PTA	377	77	46	12
Friends' Association	268	54	133	50
Prize Funds	141	29	60	43
Department Funds	49	10	8	16
Fundraising Committee	19	4	7	41
Endowment Fund	8	2	6	75
Trust Funds	0	0	0	0

5 Main sources of support for primary schools

Most of the primary schools surveyed had under 300 pupils. It was much harder for their headteachers than for others to release a teacher to make external contacts with companies and trusts in working hours. Again and again they told us: 'I am a teaching head; I have no time to spare unless I neglect more important things – like education!' Unsurprisingly the primary schools showed themselves strongly dependent on financial and volunteer fundraising help from parents.

Parents and friends

We looked first to see how many primary schools regarded their Parent Teacher Associations, Home–School Associations or Friends' non-LEA Associations as their main source of funding. We also wondered whether the village nature of many of the schools in the rural area would create greater closeness, or conversely, whether the need to travel longer distances would decrease parental activity. In each of the paired rural and urban areas, one was markedly more active than others in involving parent and community groups in fundraising. This suggests that the problems of bringing parents together in rural schools are no greater, or no easier, than bringing them together in the inner city or across the suburbs, with much depending on the attitudes and volunteer management skills of local headteachers, and on the ability of parents to respond.

Some heads challenged us not to make over-simple assumptions. One commented on the fact that, in a previous school, he had struggled to involve inner-city parents, and thought that was the only problem. Now, in a more prosperous area, he faced a different version of the same problem: many children were delivered to school by childminders or au-pairs; their dual career parents were too busy or too tired to help with fundraising.

We did not directly ask for the amounts donated by parents alone, since many schools now find this difficult to chart in their voluntary accounts. However, the general impression was that, at the lower end of the fundraising spectrum, parents were the main donors to primary schoools. Large capital sums, bid funding and major charitable or business donations were more likely to come, if at all, through the intervention of the headteacher or other senior member of staff.

TABLE 5.1
Primary schools naming HSAs/PTAs or Friends' Associations as their main supporters

By area		
Area A/r Respondents: 76	No. of schools	% area sample
Home–School or Parent–Teacher Association	37	49
Friends' Association	29	38
Total	66	87
Area B/r Respondents: 93		
Home–School or Parent–Teacher Association	35	38
Friends' Association	27	29
Total	62	67
Area C/u Respondents: 112		
Home–School or Parent–Teacher Association	64	57
Friends' Association	28	25
Total	92	82
Area D/u Respondents: 211		
Home–School or Parent–Teacher Association	97	46
Friends' Association	38	18
Total	135	64
	No. of schools	% total sample(492)
Total	355	72

The bid culture

We asked the schools about the range of financial and in-kind support that was now, theoretically at least, available to them from non-LEA and non-parental sources. There were three main possibilities: funding from governmental or agency sources as part of the new 'bid culture', often involving the creation of various local partnerships and the support of a local authority; applications to charitable trusts and the development of a funding or other relationship with a business partner. (The GEST/Standards Fund, virtually an aspect of mainstream funding featured in the questionnaire, is excluded from the table below, since almost all schools acknowledged its important contribution to their school.) We have left in the SRB/Challenge funds as an reminder of their importance to schools in areas where other forms of additional funding are not easy to find.

Companies and charitable trusts

The list in Table 5.2 shows the sources of non-parental external support most often mentioned by responding schools, in priority order. The table draws attention to the fact that many companies, in particular, now provide assistance in the form of gifts in kind, not cash. Companies and trusts, though high on the table, were named by not more than 15% of the total sample. Primary school headteachers made many heart-felt comments on the time taken by fundraising by bid and grant application, and about the bitter disappointments of being turned down with little or no explanation. Arguably it was the schools that did not name any of these sources that were most significant.

TABLE 5.2
External funders supporting primary schools

Frequency of naming	No. of schools	Gifts in kind
Companies	73	83
Diocesan Funds	72	5
Trust Funding	69	16
European Funds	37	5
SRB	31	3
Community Chest	30	7
TECs	26	12
Arts Council	23	5
Education Business Partnerships	23	19
Sports Council	13	34
Safer Cities	9	2
Department of Health	7	10
City Challenge	7	2
Urban District Council	2	1

Area differences

The most notable difference across the four areas was the absence of charitable trusts from the top five funders in Area D/u. This was expected, since it reflected the relatively low levels of trust activity in this area generally, but it had the effect of lowering the overall position of the charitable trusts, which topped the other three area lists. In Area D/u, where both trust and parental funding was limited, there was a greater reliance on Diocesan, SRB and TEC funding. In Area A/r, the high position of Arts Council funding, second on the list, was unexpected.

6 The impact of the National Lottery on primary schools

The first five 'good causes'

Of the total primary sample, only 34 (7%) said that their schools had already benefited from the various National Lottery Funds. Since these grants were not available directly to schools but will have required careful negotiation of a partnership, the small numbers of primary schools involved were not surprising. The sixteen primary schools that achieved grants for Sports; twelve for the Arts; three for Millennium funding; two from the Charities Board and one from the Heritage Board did well.

The New Opportunities Fund (NOF): the sixth good cause

Table 6 shows 50% of primary schools in England intending to apply for the New Opportunities Fund, the new 'sixth cause' of the National Lottery, intended to fund non-statutory after-school homework centres, clubs and other innovative educational projects. Since NOF is planned to benefit 25% of all primary schools, the figures in Table 6 suggest that primary schools have odds of 2:1 on success with their application – well worth the effort.

There was an unsurprising correlation between the schools intending to apply for NOF funding, and those feeling satisfied that they had sufficient information. A significant proportion felt that they had insufficient information to make a firm judgement.

Area B/r reported only 40% interest in NOF compared with 47%–50% interest elsewhere. This very slight regional variation is significant only alongside other evidence suggesting that this rural area was more reluctant than others to take the fundraising plunge, and when it did so, was more reluctant than others to set itself high targets.

TABLE 6

Primary schools intending to apply for the New Opportunities Fund

	No. of schools	% total sample (492)
Yes	229	47
No	185	38
Non-response	78	15

Satisfaction with information supplied about the New Opportunities Fund

	No. of schools	% total sample (492)
Sufficient	260	53
Insufficient	182	37
Non-response	50	10

By area: intention to apply

	No. of schools	% area sample
Area A/r		
Yes	36	47
Area B/r		
Yes	37	40
Area C/u		
Yes	56	50
Area D/u		
Yes	100	47

7 Factors affecting primary school fundraising

Type and category of school

It was evident from their development appeals that some of the highest amounts raised by primary schools were for voluntary school new building purposes, and supported by Diocesan funds. However, we also wanted to investigate the widely held assumption that grant maintained (now mostly foundation) schools raise more money than others.

In each of the two paired areas, one area had notably higher numbers of foundation schools. Area A/r had one foundation primary school; Area B/r had ten; Area C/u had two; Area D/u (which was large) had ten. Table 7.1 suggests that foundation primary schools, although not raising significantly higher amounts than the rest of the primary respondents, were doing better in the £5,000–£10,000 band.

TABLE 7.1

Financial support raised by GM primary schools, compared with all schools in the sample, 1997–98

	GM schools (Respondents: 23)	%	cf Non-GM schools (Respondents: 450)	%
Less than £1,000	4	17	89	20
£1,001–£5,000	10	43	278	62
£5,001–£10,000	6	26	58	13
£10,001–£15,000	2	9	15	3
£15,001–£25,000	0	0	6	1
£25,001–£35,000	1	4	0	0
£35,001–£50,000	0	0	2	0.4
£50,001–£100,000	0	0	2	0.4

Area differences

Many primary schools explained their lack of fundraising success in terms of the type of area in which they were situated; they often took opposite (and not necessarily contradictory) positions: 'We find it hard because we are only a small rural school in the middle of nowhere'... 'because we are an inner city school in an area under extreme social pressure'... 'because people think we are already very advantaged', and so on. Both the rural areas surveyed contained towns with pockets of poverty, whilst both 'urban' areas were fringed with prosperous suburbs and commuter countryside. Nevertheless, it seemed worth testing the proposition that area made a major difference.

As Tables 7.2 shows, the similarities between primary schools in each of the four areas surveyed were generally more striking than the differences, leading us to conclude that the rural/urban distinction is not as significant as other factors, such as whether or not the parents are employed and have goodwill towards the school and disposable income, or whether an individual has the time and knowledge required to make a successful bid or application. Overall, Area C/u had the fewest schools (11%) raising less than £1,000 a year; it is also overall the most prosperous and economically active of the four areas. Area D/u, the northern area, had the highest numbers of poor schools but also some of the richest.

TABLE 7.2

By area:
Financial support raised by primary schools in addition to the main school budget 1997–98

	Area A/r		Area B/r		Area C/u		Area D/u	
	No. of schools (Respondents: 74)	%	No. of schools (Respondents: 89)	%	No. of schools (Respondents: 105)	%	No. of schools (Respondents: 205)	%
Less than £1,000	13	18	19	21	12	11	49	24
£1,001–£5,000	51	67	54	61	65	62	118	58
£5,001–£10,000	7	9	12	13	21	20	24	12
£10,001–£15,000	1	1	1	1	5	5	10	5
£15,001–£25,000	1	1	1	1	2	2	2	1
£25,001–£35,000	0	0	1	1	0	0	0	0
£35,001–£50,000	1	1	0	0	0	0	1	0.5
£50,001–£100,000	0	0	1	1	0	0	1	0.5

8 Disadvantage, deprivation and primary school fundraising

Whilst aware of the caveats, we used the numbers of pupils receiving free school meals as an easily measurable indicator of deprivation and disadvantage. It was immediately noticeable that, even after allowing for their greater size, the two urban areas had more schools with over 25% of pupils in receipt of school meals. 10 of the 11 schools reporting that no pupils were in receipt of free school meals were in Area B/r.

TABLE 8.1

Numbers of primary schools with pupils in receipt of free school meals
Respondents: 411

	No. of schools	%
None	11	3
less than 10% free meals	162	39
10%–25% free meals	124	30
25%–50% free meals	60	15
50%–75% free meals	46	11
75%–100% free meals	8	2

	Area A/r	Area B/r	Area C/u	Area D/u
	No. of schools	No. of schools	No. of schools	No. of schools
None	0	10	0	1
less than 10% free meals	21	48	52	41
10%–25% free meals	0	24	30	70
25%–50% free meals	0	7	18	35
50%–75% free meals	0	2	9	35
75%–100% free meals	0	1	0	7

Amounts raised

Many of the schools with high numbers of pupils in receipt of free school meals did not reply to the 'amounts raised' question, in some cases because they had nothing to report. Table 8.2 compares firstly fundraising results in schools with high and low deprivation levels. It uses the free school meals indicators 50%–100% and less than 10% to define high and low, and then, in the right-hand column, enables a comparison to be made between the results of the 'high deprivation' schools and the overall primary schools response (as in Table 1). It is striking that few primary schools with over 50% of pupils on free school meals were raising more than £5,000 a year, and far more (56%) were raising less than £1,000.

TABLE 8.2

Amounts raised in primary schools responding, with high and low percentages of free school meals

	50%–100%	% resp	Under 10%	% resp.	cf. Table 1	total sample %
	(Respondents: 52)		(Respondents: 172)		(Respondents: 473)	
Less than £1,000	29	56	17	10	93	20
£1,001–£5,000	20	38	107	62	288	61
£5,001–£10,000	1	2	39	23	64	14
£10,001–£15,000	1	2	6	3	17	4
£15,001–£25,000	1	2	3	2	6	1
£25,001–£35,000	0	0	0	0	1	0.2
£35,001–£50,000	0	0	0	0	2	0.4
£50,001–£100,000	0	0	0	0	2	0.4

Company and trust support

Although the number of schools providing this information is too small to produce a reliable national picture, Table 8.3 is striking evidence that, in the primary schools surveyed, trust and company support appeared to go overwhelmingly to the more advantaged schools. No school in the entire sample with over 75% on free school meals reported that they had received support from either companies or trusts.

Area A/r had, overall, hardly any support from either companies or trusts.

Areas B/r and C/u, one rural and one urban, both had relatively high input from trusts and companies, reflecting local trust traditions and a more prosperous economy. Even here, the strong bias towards the more advantaged schools was evident.

In Area D/u, a city with little tradition of trust giving, few schools of any kind benefited in this way. However, SRB funding went to 8 schools with over 50% of pupils in receipt of free school meals, but to no schools with under 10% free school meals.

TABLE 8.3
Company and trust support of schools with more than 50% of pupils in receipt of free school meals, compared with schools with fewer than 10% of pupils in receipt of free school meals.

	Company support	%	Trust support	%
Over 50% free school meals	5	10	3	6
Respondents 52				
Under 10% free school meals	25	15	31	18
Respondents 172				
Area A/r				
Over 50% free school meals	0	–	–	0
Under 10% free school meals	0	–	–	2
Area B/r				
Over 50% free school meals	1	–	–	0
Under 10% free school meals	8	–	–	12
Area C/u				
Over 50% free school meals	1	–	–	1
Under 10% free school meals	11	–	–	16
Area D/u				
Over 50% free school meals	3	–	–	2
Under 10% free school meals	6	–	–	1

9 Difficulties and information needs of primary schools

We asked schools for their further comments on fundraising problems and needs, and whether there were any local problems.

31 of the 55 primary schools responding to this question said they experienced difficulties in funding. 24 said they had no difficulties, though some modified this by saying it was because they didn't make fundraising a priority.

When schools were asked about their own local problems in fundraising, many mentioned the fact that their area had little or no active company involvement in schools, or indeed few active local employers. This emerges, again not surprisingly, as one of most significant factors in fundraising disadvantage for many primary schools: low levels of local corporate activity and investment is typically accompanied by high unemployment amongst parents.

Table 9, which is reproduced in both the maintained primary and secondary school findings, presents a summary of the main difficulties expressed by teachers in maintained schools; their own written comments are also reproduced more fully elsewhere. The order of listing mirrors approximately the frequency with which each problem was voiced.

TABLE 9.1

General fundraising problems

Lack of time
Takes a disproportionate amount of time for the amounts raised
Direct level of support to schools should be raised
Core funding is now below acceptable levels
Don't believe education should be funded through charities
Need advice on fundraising
Too many other pressures

Local fundraising problems

Decline of, or lack of, local business
Difficult to access industrial funding
Companies are looking for something in return
Competition with other schools
Deprived area/high unemployment/parental poverty
Parents/community uninterested
Decline in number of willing volunteers
Need for local training
Inner city school
Not a failing school, therefore do not qualify for certain types of support
Rural area/school
Not an inner city school
Outer/rural/working class schools often overlooked
Not a socially deprived area
Too few supporters; school is not in a prosperous area
High unemployment; parental poverty

Difficulties that schools found in raising money from external agencies

Lack of companies/industry in area; no SRB status
Form-filling and bureaucracy of the application process
Charitable trusts' criteria are difficult to satisfy; need expertise
Difficulty in raising matched funding
Bids are daunting
Too many bids to make; too much competition for them
Bid and similar funds do not always match the needs of the school
Intimidating process; too difficult
Not enough information on grant sources
Don't know criteria for success
Competition between schools; too many chasing too little
No success, unlucky, often turned down, discouraged
Need access and contacts to make it happen
Paperwork is over complex; form-filling bureaucracy

Information needs

388 (79%) of the responding primary schools told us that they felt in need of further fundraising information and training, with 89 (18%) indicating either that they already knew or did not want to. Curiously, 409 then went on to identify the type of training they would prefer.

TABLE 9.2

Preferred form of information: primary schools.
Respondents: 409

	No. of schools	% total sample (492)
Information on fundraising sources	273	55
Training courses	96	20
Conferences	40	8

10 Primary school fundraising for other causes

We asked all schools about the amounts raised for charities and other community causes, not for themselves. The replies were encouraging for those who fear that young people no longer give to charity. Touchingly, where the amounts raised for the schools themselves were generally rounded, the amounts quoted by the primary schools as raised for charity were often precise and clearly the result of careful counting: £1,260.08, £486.17 etc. However, we begin with a warning to over-eager charity fundraisers.

Schools and charity fundraisers

Table 10.1, which is also reproduced in the secondary school findings, lists in order of frequency of naming, the main comments made by schools about charity fundraising and charity fundraisers. It gives some insight into how best to approach a school, for example, with either a really entertaining activity for young people, a thoughtful contribution to the curriculum or an offer of a longer-term Education Charity Partnership between the school and the voluntary organisation. Charities are now frequently invited to share the profits from an event with the school itself. What are not welcomed are empty tins and stickers, unsolicited phonecalls or other insistent pressures and distractions.

TABLE 10.1

Schools' comments on fundraising for non-school charities

Too many requests received
Charities expect too much too often
Educational value is important
Keen on events (eg. Comic Relief; Children in Need)
Important to raise awareness of others
Very important/part of the school's ethos
Getting harder, only prepared to do joint fundraising: percentage for the school
Need to balance fundraising for school with needs of others
Need to balance local and national charities
Specific projects only, must be learning based or fun
Choose both local and national charities
Importance of local charities
Pupils' altruism is central
Choose local, national and international charities
Like topical charities, for curriculum input
Time consuming
Easier to fundraise for non-school charities than for school itself

Primary school giving

Table 10.2 shows the high response to this question from primary schools, which took this obligation more seriously than any other sector surveyed, clearly regarding it as an important element in their personal and social curriculum and in school life.

Area differences

It seemed likely that the poorer inner city areas might raise less for charity than others. Whilst it was true that a smaller percentage of schools in the two urban areas raised money for other charities, the vast majority of schools engaged in activities of this kind.

TABLE 10.2

Primary schools raising money for charities and local community causes
Respondents: 492

	No. of schools	%
Yes	452	92
No	35	7

Table 10.3 shows the amounts raised by area, and in total across the sample. Whilst it was true that a smaller percentage of schools in the two urban areas raised money for other charities, the vast majority of schools engaged in activities of this kind.

TABLE 10.3

Amounts raised for charity and community causes in primary schools, by area

Area A/r	No. schools responding	% area response	Amounts raised
Respondents: 76	69	91	£
Amount for local community:			19,050
Amount for other charities:			37,362
Total:			56,412
Average per school responding:			818
Area B/r			
Respondents: 93	84	90	£
Amount for community			23,491
Amount for charities:			52,096
Total:			75,587
Average per school responding:			900
Area C/u			
Respondents: 112	99	88	£
Amount for community			11,835
Amount for charities			59,171
Total:			71,006
Average per school responding:			717
Area D/u			
Respondents: 211	185	88	£
Amount for community:			58,924
amount for charitie			131,949
Total:			190,873
Average per school responding:			1,032
Total raised by responding schools (437):			£393,878
Average for all primary in these four areas: (Assuming that the non-responding schools raised no funds for these purposes)			£801

Total amount raised by primary schools for others

Finally, we estimate the average total per primary school in the areas surveyed, from which we reach the conclusion that primary schools in England are likely to be raising almost £15 million a year for charities, 19% of the amount they raise for themselves. Although this high percentage to a degree reflects the overall lower amounts raised for themselves by primary schools, their contribution to charities and community causes is a record of which they can be justly proud, and one that confirms the fact, well-known to charities, that proportionately the needy give more than the rich.

FINDINGS

FUNDRAISING IN SECONDARY SCHOOLS IN ENGLAND

This survey of 419 maintained secondary schools in England was carried out in June–August 1999.

MAIN FINDINGS

How much secondary schools raise

Of the secondary schools responding:
- 5% were raising less than £1,000 or nothing at all;
- 49% were raising more than £10,000 a year;
- of these: 3% were raising between £250,000–£500,000;
- the highest proportion of secondary schools (28%) was raising between £1,000–£5,000 a year;
- a much wider spread of funds was indicated than in the primary schools survey, though not as wide as the spread of funds raised by independent schools.

An indicative estimate of the amounts raised by all secondary schools in England can be made on the basis of these figures. Schools were not asked to display the precise amount raised, but were asked into which of a number of bands their fundraising fell. On the assumption that the responding schools were representative and that, on average, their fundraised income lay at the middle of the band named, national figures as follows are indicated for maintained secondary schools in England:

- £143 million a year (or an average of £4,000 a school, or around £47 per pupil) raised by maintained English secondary schools from sources outside their main school budget.

It is important to note that this average is heavily influenced by the large sums raised in the 3% of secondary schools with annual voluntary income of over £250,000 a year, many of which will have raised £100,000 towards specialist school status.

- if that 3% is excluded, the average per secondary school in the remaining 97% falls to about £30,000.
- if the highest fundraising 10% of schools is excluded, the figure per secondary school drops to a more typical figure of £17,400, or around £20 per pupil.

Main sources of support for secondary schools

- companies were the highest non-mainstream/LEA and non-parental funders of secondary schools;
- parents nevertheless continued to be the first call for fundraising support, at least for the great majority of secondary schools;
- 56% of secondary schools surveyed were intending to apply to the New Opportunities Fund.

Factors affecting secondary school fundraising include:

- the availability to the schools of up-to-date information and the time and expertise required to raise significant sums from specialist bids, including European and SRB/Challenge funds, charitable trusts, company donors and sponsors;
- the involvement of parents and others and their ability to provide financial support (noting that involvement does not necessarily imply personal donations);

- the presence, or not, in the locality of companies and charitable trusts willing to provide financial help, advice or gifts in kind, and their policies and selection procedures;
- girls' schools found more difficulty in raising money than boys' schools;
- foundation schools, many of which were until recently grant maintained schools and grammar schools, were amongst the most active fundraisers; some but not all raised relatively high amounts;
- some of the highest fundraising secondary schools were community schools with high levels of parental and/or external support;
- 92% of English secondary schools responding said they needed more information and training on sources and methods of fundraising;
- 40% of English secondary schools responding said they had insufficient information about the New Opportunities Fund.

Secondary school fundraising for charitable and community causes

Of the secondary schools responding:
- 90% of English secondary schools surveyed said they raised money for charities and community causes;
- £1.6 million a year (an average of around £4,000 a school) was being raised by all secondary schools surveyed. We counted the non-responding schools as raising zero income for others.

An indicative national estimate, if these samples are assumed to be representative, is that:
- all secondary schools in England may be raising over £14 million a year for charities and local community causes (10% of the amount they raise for themselves).

HOW THE RESEARCH WAS CARRIED OUT

This survey of maintained secondary schools in England was carried out by the Directory of Social Change in 1999. In almost all cases financial information applies to the year 1997–98.

Sample

In June 1999 questionnaires were sent out to 1,591 schools, i.e. about 45% of the 3,567 secondary schools in England and including 147 local authorities. Special schools and independent secondary schools were also mailed; they are commented on separately but do not form part of this survey.

Response rate

We received, in total, 419 replies (26% of the sample and 12% of all secondary schools in England) from the maintained secondary schools. There were 9 local authorities from which no replies were received, leaving schools from 138 authorities included in the sample for analysis.

Data

Where figures used in the tables below are not based on the total number of responding schools, ('the respondents') figure from which the table is derived is stated. Where figures have been rounded, there may be minor discrepancies between the sum of the constituent parts and the totals as shown.

RESULTS

1 How much is raised by secondary schools

The amounts raised by secondary schools in England cover a wide spread. Just over half the secondary schools surveyed raised under £10,000 a year. Of these, 33% were raising less than £5,000. However 10% of the schools surveyed here were raising over £100,000 a year. The survey results, if representative of all maintained secondary schools in England, suggest that the total raised is around £136 million a year, with a small number also setting high targets for longer-term development appeals. 32 secondary schools (8%) failed to answer the question: 'How much do you raise?' They have been excluded from the respondent base in Table 1 because we had no knowledge of whether these schools were exceptionally high and discreet fundraisers or had no voluntary income to report.

Schools raising the larger amounts include those that had recently generated £100,000 as the match funding required to change the status of their school to that of a specialist school. Of the schools that had raised £50,000 to £250,000, 10 were also running a development appeal, aiming to raise between £60,000 to £635,000. Of the 5% that said they raised less than £1,000, many reported raising nothing at all: their only source of income was their LEA school budget share.

TABLE 1

Financial support raised by secondary schools, in addition to the main school budget 1997–98. Respondents 376

	No. of schools	%
Less than £1,000	17	5
£1,001–£5,000	104	28
£5,001–£10,000	71	19
£10,001–£15,000	32	9
£15,001–£25,000	43	11
£25,001–£35,000	15	4
£35,001–£50,000	22	6
£50,001–£100,000	32	9
£100,001–250,000	29	8
£250,001–£500,000	11	3

2 What secondary schools raise money for

Replies to this question gave us a vivid picture both of the secondary schools' own perceived needs and of the external pressures on teachers to fundraise. Computers, music and sports equipment topped the secondary school list, followed by books, transport and voluntary support of school trips. One school said its governors (otherwise rarely mentioned beings) had helped raise the required 15% matched funding for grant aided projects supported by the DfEE.

We also gave secondary school headteachers the opportunity to name 'other items' for which funds were raised. Most secondary schools were raising money for more than one item, typically between three and six. A few were optimistically tackling wish lists of ten, eleven or even thirteen items or projects, all at once.

In addition to those shown in the listing below, other projects for which secondary schools were raising funds included: social areas for year groups; CCTV equipment; a careers questionnaire for year 10/11; ceramics kilns; first aid facilities; a telescope; picnic tables; a reward scheme for pupils; a DoE award; a business studies and food technology suite; residential study support; transport to sports and curriculum linked activities; assertive discipline prizes, and the purchase of secondhand computers from local businesses.

TABLE 2.1
What secondary schools raise money for

Items	No. of schools	% total sample (419)
Computers	210	50
Music equipment	207	49
Sports equipment	186	44
Books	177	42
Library	161	38
Minibuses	159	38
Trips	150	36
School buildings	100	24
Sports/music tours	99	24
Furniture	56	13
Playground	55	13
School grounds	47	11
Specialist arts help	47	11
Gym	24	6
Swimming pool	14	3
Parents' facilities	5	1
Stationery	5	1
Teachers' salaries	1	0.2

TABLE 2.2
'Other' items named by secondary schools as fundraising targets
Respondents: 63

Items	No. of schools
Specialist schools status	6
Video/AV equipment	6
Furniture	5
Decoration (upgrade/modify/curtains etc.)	4
IT Equipment	4
Science equipment	3
Staging	3
Technology	3
Sports facilities	3
Company promotion vouchers	3
Disabled facilities	3
Music school	2
Art	2
Specific departmental equipment	2
Security	2
Transport	2
Support for poor families	2
Textiles	1
Work experience	1
Homework clubs	1

3 How secondary schools raise money

We asked if any of eight likely approaches to fundraising had been employed. Secondary schools, like primary schools, still appeared to rely heavily on event-fundraising, which often had a second motive, to bring parents and the community into the school. However, the secondary schools also typically used a wider range of fundraising methods than their primary school colleagues. For example, 42% of secondary schools, compared with 25% of primary schools, claimed to be actively seeking sponsorship. Although as with primary schools there was some ambiguity about how the schools interpreted this term, secondary schools were more likely to assume this referred to commercial sponsorships by local businesses, not sponsorship of individuals undertaking an activity.

38% of secondary schools were engaged in trading activities, and some of the highest fundraisers placed particular emphasis on this as a main source of income. We did not specifically ask about the 'Schools Voucher' schemes, a relatively recent but now ubiquitous company marketing device employed by many supermarkets and newspapers, but several schools commented on this development, positively and negatively. Larger schools found it a relatively easy way to raise funds; small schools felt they could never raise enough vouchers to gain anything worthwhile, but still felt bound to take part, with all the administration that entailed, when faced by eagerly donated scraps of paper. Although marketing based campaigns of this kind put commercial pressure on parents and pupils to use certain stores, or to purchase certain newspapers or goods, this was seen as a marginally better course than pressing poor families to give money directly or to make purchases they didn't want.

A small number of secondary schools were experimenting with 'affinity' credit cards, though as yet with little evidence of success. Secondary schools notably made greater use of tax-effective means of giving, with, for example, 23% of the sample using covenants, compared with only 3% of the primary schools. (Meanwhile, 56% of their counterparts in the independent sector operated school covenant schemes.) The balance between covenanting and Gift Aid may change as the Chancellor's recently announced tax concessions for charities begin to make it easier to give small one-off charity donations tax-effectively. Now that small one-off amounts can be tax-effectively donated through Gift Aid, there may be less pressure on supporters to enter into the long-term commitment of a covenant.

TABLE 3.1
The most frequently reported fundraising methods in secondary schools

	No. of schools naming	% total sample (419)
Events	264	63
Sponsorship	171	41
Trading	155	37
200 Clubs	140	33
Affinity cards	17	4
Tax-effective giving		
Covenants	97	23
Gift Aid	44	11
Legacies	12	3

Development Appeals

There were various objects of longer-term school development appeals, still relatively new in the maintained sector. We were interested to learn what types and categories of secondary school had development appeals, what targets the schools were setting themselves and for what purposes.

Many, but not all of the schools with development appeals were ambitious fundraisers: across the sample, appeal targets ranged between £2,500 to £2,750,000, with nearly 20 schools aiming for £100,000. Success rates varied; a number of appeals had just started. Most had already raised over £5,000 and the most successful to date had already raised £1,750,000.

Although most of the schools with development appeals were comprehensives, this reflects the structure of the education system (c.3,403 comprehensive:166 grammar schools in England at the time of writing). If the picture in Table 3.4 also reflects the national picture, this suggests that 2% of comprehensive schools compared with 10% of grammar schools have development appeals. Of the 85 schools that told us they had development appeals and were GM schools, 12 schools (14%) said they were also grammar schools

TABLE 3.2
Secondary schools with development appeals.
Respondents: 406

	No. of schools	%
Yes	85	21
No	321	79
Schools with development appeals		
Community/county	45	11
GM	21	5
Voluntary Aided	13	3
Voluntary Controlled	3	0.7
Special Agreement	1	0.2
Language Agreement	1	0.2
Changing to Specialist status (Sept 99)	1	0.2
By type:		
Comprehensive	71	17
Grammar	20	5

What the appeals were for

As Table 3.3. shows, over 20% of the secondary schools responding were targeting their appeals on sports facilities. Other named fundraising objectives were imaginative and extensive. Schools were developing food technology facilities; common rooms; a fitness suite (possibly also as a source of hiring income); a school chapel; a learning resource centre; a Shakespeare Festival; international education projects; music rehearsal areas, and a Millennium Footpath development.

TABLE 3.3
Frequently named objects of development appeals in secondary schools.
Respondents: 85

Purpose of appeal	No. of schools
Sports activities and facilities	20
Specialist schools status	17
School buildings	12
ICT/technology	8
Arts facilities	8
Minibus	6
Library	5
Anniversary appeals	2
For matching schemes	2

4 How fundraising is managed in secondary schools

We wanted to know two things: who organised the fundraising in secondary schools and who held, controlled (and so was accountable for) the funds themselves. Many of the PTAs/HSAs, regularly recognised as the main additional source of school funding, are constituted as independent charities with their own management committees. Yet interestingly they were not always perceived as having the main responsibility for the fundraising or the funds.

Who organises the work

Headteachers and parents were strongly in the lead, with school governors notably quite a long way down the list. Since they are ultimately responsible for the schools' financial affairs, this absence from a table compiled by headteachers was striking.

Unlike the primary schools, the secondary schools regularly named the deputy heads as main organisers of fundraising. It is not uncommon for a deputy head to be responsible for fundraising, including grant and bid applications. Many deputy heads have become highly experienced fundraisers, but at a time-cost to other duties.

The percentages shown in Table 4.1 compare the number of replies with the total sample of responding schools. Many schools showed more than one person as having 'main responsibility' for fundraising, usually the headteacher and the parents. This is an admirable situation, provided individual responsibilities are clearly defined, in particular who decides how the funds are used. Several secondary schools named more than one person, usually headteacher and parents, or the headteacher and senior team, as have prime responsibility for fundraising.

TABLE 4.1
Persons named as having prime responsibility for secondary school fundraising.
Respondents: 204

	No. of schools	%
Headteacher	96	47
Deputy head	28	14
Department head	6	3
Governors	4	2
Parents	54	26
Development officer	3	1
Resource manager	12	6
External fundraiser	1	0.5

Development officer, resource manager, fundraiser, fundraising consultant

43 schools said that they had a resource manager in post. In 31 of these schools this person had the main responsibility for organising the school's fundraising. Five schools said the development officer's responsibility was shared with the deputy headteacher, and in one case with the headteacher. One school had combined the post of deputy headteacher with that of resource manager.

Two schools named the resource manager and parents as having the main fundraising organising role. Interestingly, only one school named jointly the resource manager, headteacher, deputy headteacher and parents as having the main responsibility for fundraising.

Who holds the funds

We also wanted to know who was accountable for the various funds held by schools. Unsurprisingly the 'School Fund' tops the list of contributors, since in almost all schools the School Fund becomes the resting place for monies from sources beyond the statutory; these may include private funds such as money collected towards a school holiday, or charitable donations from an individual or charitable trust.

Table 4.2 indicates the general awareness of charity law within the schools and amongst their supporters. PTA and similar school support organisations in England seemed remarkably well aware of their obligation to register with the Charity Commission if they were constituted as independent charities exclusively for the advancement of education, and if their income exceeded the £1,000 annual income threshold. Whether or not the headteachers and governing bodies who controlled the schools' voluntary income held in a School Fund were as aware of the reporting and accountability requirements for school funds held on trust is more doubtful and, given the present lack of clear guidance, entirely understandable. This issue is discussed at greater length in the Introduction (see p9).

Again, the percentages in Table 4.2 indicate the proportion of schools naming a particular fund or fund-holder, compared with the total number of schools in the sample; there are overlaps, hence percentages do not total 100. The final right-hand column shows the registered charities in column four as a percentage of the similar funds named in column one. It gives only a rough guide to the general levels of awareness; many charitable PTAs and other organisations hold few or no assets and do not approach the level at which small charity registration becomes a requirement.

TABLE 4.2

Funds contributing to and holding secondary school fundraising income

	Fund contributes financially		Fund is a registered charity	
	No. schools	% total sample	No of schools	Col. 3 as % col. 1
HSA/PTA	284	68	132	46
Friends Association	120	29	40	33
Department funds	117	28	4	3
Prize Funds	97	23	19	20
Fundraising Committee	71	17	8	11
Trust Funds	69	17	50	72
Endowment Fund	29	7	22	76

5 Main sources of support for secondary schools

Parents and friends

We looked to see how many schools regarded their PTAs, Home–School Associations or Friends' Associations as their main non-LEA source of funding. Secondary schools frequently complain that it is harder to involve parents at this stage: more are working full-time and pupils are reluctant to see their parents invading their school space. However, a high percentage (60%) of the responding schools perceived parents to be their major source of non-LEA funding, on a far bigger scale than their counterparts in independent schools, but much less than the primary schools, (which typically reported parents as prime fundraisers in over 80% of schools). Once the school aspires to raise amounts over £50,000 the fundraisers need to have more specialist skills and knowledge, particularly of bidding and large-scale appeal fundraising and the main responsibility for raising these major amounts of money usually passes to the school itself.

TABLE 5.1

Secondary schools naming HSAs/PTAs or Friends' Associations as their main supporters

	No of schools	% total sample
Home–School or Parent–Teacher Association	201	48
Friends' Association	51	12

The bid culture

We asked the schools about the range of financial and 'in kind' support that was now theoretically available to them from non-LEA and non-parental sources. Table 5.2 shows some of the main sources of non-LEA funding, non-parental funding on which the schools could draw. The GEST/Standards Fund, virtually an aspect of mainstream funding, featured in the questionnaire but is excluded from Table 5.2 since almost all schools acknowledged its important contribution. We have left in the SRB/Challenge funds as a reminder of their importance to schools in areas where other forms of additional funding are not easy to find.

The list on the left of Table 5.2 shows the sources of support most often mentioned by responding schools, in priority order. The table draws attention to the fact that many companies, in particular, provide assistance in the form of gifts in kind, not cash.

Companies and charitable trusts

Grant making by trusts to schools was quite widespread, with over 25% of the sample saying they had received support from this source. Individual schools named a number of trusts, including Letchworth Garden City Heritage Foundation, Lord's Feoffees, John Lyon Trust, Glaxo Wellcome, and most commonly, Prince's Trust.

50 schools listed a range of other supporters that had helped the school, and seven noted that no additional funders had contributed to the school. Sports funders were a popular source of extra support, with the Foundation for Sport and the Arts, Lords Taverners, Barclays Bank Sports Initiative, the Lawn Tennis Association, a local cricket club (Lancashire) and National Lottery Sports Fund all helping schools with facilities.

Table 5.2 clearly indicates the high reliance of secondary schools on business support, whether from local or national companies, which supported about 40% of schools surveyed, or from the Education Business Partnerships (EBPs), which supported about 37% of the schools surveyed. In the Education Action Zones the level of reliance is likely to be even heavier and may benefit the schools that find other sources of support hard to access.

TABLE 5.2

External funders supporting secondary schools

Frequency of naming	Financial support	Gifts in kind
Companies	165	115
Education Business Partnerships	151	49
TECs	142	23
Charitable trusts	115	9
Single Regeneration Budget (SRB)	79	8
European Funds	74	5
Sports Council	62	12
Arts Council	34	5
Community Chest	25	1
Diocesan Funds (not buildings)	24	3
City Challenge	12	1
Department of Health	8	2
Safer Cities	6	2
Urban Development Corporation	2	1
Task Force	1	0

6 The impact of the National Lottery on secondary schools

The first five 'good causes'

Of the total secondary school sample, 66 (16%) said that their schools had already benefited from the various National Lottery Funds. The need for 'match funding' was a common deterrent. This success rate represents a high proportion, considering that the funding was only available to schools through developed partnerships with others, demonstrating the community benefit of the project.

TABLE 6.1

Secondary Schools that had already successfully raised funds from the National Lottery
Respondents: 66

	No. of schools
Arts	15
Charities	3
Heritage	0
Sports	43
Millennium	5

The New Opportunities Fund (NOF): the sixth good cause

The NOF aims to benefit 'at least half of all secondary schools and a quarter of all primary schools'. If the percentage in Table 5.2 is typical of the country as a whole, secondary schools stand a high chance of success when applying for NOF funds – the odds are worth the effort of application.

A significant proportion of those who did not plan to apply or who were undecided said they had received insufficient information to make a firm judgement.

TABLE 6.2
Secondary schools intending to apply for the New Opportunities Fund.

	No. of schools	% total sample (419)
Yes	231	55
No	132	31

Satisfaction with information supplied about the New Opportunities Fund

	No. of schools	% total sample
Sufficient	223	53
Insufficient	155	36

7 Factors affecting secondary school fundraising

Type and category of school

Voluntary aided schools have long had to contribute towards capital buildings and external maintenance costs; it was evident that some of the highest amounts raised had been for building purposes and supported by Diocesan funds.

We also wanted to investigate the widely-held assumption that grant maintained schools and grammar schools raise more money than others. The 69 grant maintained schools in the survey (almost all now foundation schools, although some reverted to voluntary aided status) represented 10% of the 667 grant maintained schools existing at the time of survey. The 20 grammar schools responding represent 12% of the 166 English grammar schools existing at the time of survey. Table 7.2 appears to show that GM/foundation and grammar schools are not raising notably higher sums than others, although they score marginally higher in the band £5,000–£10,000. The wide variations between schools of the same type and/or category suggests that few conclusions can be drawn from the formal structure of the school; the home circumstances of the pupils are probably a better indicator. Some GM schools were, however, markedly more active in setting up development appeals.

TABLE 7.1
No. of GM secondary schools responding

Numbers of schools	% total sample
75	18

No. of secondary grammar schools responding

Numbers of schools	% total sample
20	5

Of these:
No. of GM grammar schools responding

Numbers of schools	% total sample
12	3

TABLE 7.2
Financial support raised by GM secondary schools compared with all schools in the sample, 1997–98

	GM schools	%	cf Non-GM schools	%
	(Respondents: 69)		(Respondents: 307)	
Less than £1,000	3	4	14	5
£1,001–£5,000	14	20	90	29
£5,001–£10,000	17	25	54	17
£10,001–£15,000	6	9	26	8
£15,001–£25,000	7	10	36	12
£25,001–£35,000	3	4	12	4
£35,001–£50,000	5	7	17	6
£50,001–£100,000	11	16	21	7
£100,001–£250,000	1	1	28	9
£250,001–£500,000	2	3	9	3

8 Disadvantage, deprivation and secondary school fundraising

As with primary schools, it is harder to raise money in a socially deprived area, and we wanted to explore this. Though aware of its limitations, we used the percentage of pupils receiving school meals as an indicator of disadvantage. We noticed the overall lower percentages of pupils in secondary schools receiving free school meals, which doubtless reflected the lower numbers eating on school premises.

One or two disadvantaged secondary schools, where the high numbers of pupils on free school meals reflect the general poverty of the area, raised large amounts of money, usually through their access to SRB or similar challenge funds. But this picture is far from typical. In the pockets of poverty and social deprivation that exist in rural or outer city areas where the media and company donors venture less often, many schools receive no additional help.

TABLE 8.1
Numbers of secondary schools with pupils in receipt of free school meals.
Respondents: 398

	No. of schools	%
less than 10% free meals	153	38
10%–25% free meals	146	37
25%–50% free meals	82	21
50%–75% free meals	16	4
75%–100% free meals	1	0

TABLE 8.2
Amounts raised in secondary schools responding, with high and low percentages of free school meals

	50%–100%	%	Under 10%	%	cf. all respondents	%
	(Respondents 15)		(Respondents 146)		(Respondents 376)	
Less than £1,000	3	20	0	0	17	5
£1,001–£5,000	4	27	37	25	104	28
£5,001–£10,000	3	20	32	22	71	19
£10,001–£15,000	0	0	16	11	32	9
£15,001–£25,000	2	13	17	12	43	11
£25,001–£35,000	0	0	7	5	15	4
£35,001–£50,000	1	7	12	8	22	6
£50,001–£100,000	1	7	12	8	32	9
£100,001–£250,000	1	7	9	6	29	8
£250,001–£500,000	0	0	4	3	11	3
(No amount given)	2	–	7	–	32	–

Company and trust support

Companies are less likely to invest in areas where they are not employers which, as many teachers told us, disadvantages schools and pupils in areas of high unemployment. Nevertheless, a higher proportion of secondary than primary schools received company support of various kinds and, unlike the case of the primary schools, company support did not appear heavily skewed in favour of the more 'advantaged' schools. Charitable trusts, where they support schools at all, have fewer reasons not to target the most needy. Yet the only secondary school with over 75% of pupils on free school meals received no money from either companies or trusts.

TABLE 8.3

Company and trust support for schools with more than 50% of pupils on free school meals, compared with schools on fewer than 10% of pupils on free school meals

	Company support	%	Trust support	%
Over 50% free school meals Respondents: 17	7	41	5	29
Under 10% free school meals Respondents: 153	66	43	52	34

9 Difficulties and information needs of secondary schools

When schools were asked about their own local problems in fundraising, many mentioned the fact that their area had little or no active company involvement in schools. This emerges as a significant factor in fundraising disadvantage for many secondary schools: high unemployment amongst parents is typically accompanied by low levels of local corporate investment. Although a large number of schools had raised support from a variety of different sources, a high percentage (66%) indicated that they had found difficulties. Descriptions of the difficulties were often lengthy and impassioned. Rather like some charities' views on fundraising, it seemed for many schools that it was always easier for the school in the next town or county to raise support, than it was for them. Some schools felt that they were not popular because they were not a failing school. One school felt that they had no appeal for industry as their pupils were girls aged 12 to 16. Many schools reported on their difficulties with the complexities and bureaucracy of bid and grant application procedures, and on their disillusion when these repeatedly failed.

Table 9.1 is reproduced in both the maintained primary and secondary school findings because it presents so clear a picture of the problems faced by all schools; the teachers' own comments are also reproduced more fully elsewhere.

TABLE 9.1

General fundraising problems

Lack of time
Takes a disproportionate amount of time for the amounts raised
Direct level of support to schools should be raised
Core funding is now below acceptable levels
Don't believe education should be funded through charities
Need advice on fundraising
Too many other pressures

Local fundraising problems

Decline of, or lack of, local business
Difficult to access industrial funding
Companies are looking for something in return
Competition with other schools
Deprived area/high unemployment/parental poverty
Parents/community uninterested
Decline in number of willing volunteers
Need for local training

Inner city school
Not an inner city school
Not a failing school, therefore do not qualify for certain types of support
Rural area/school
Outer/rural/working class schools often overlooked
Not a socially deprived area
Too few supporters; school is not in a prosperous area
High unemployment; parental poverty

Difficulties that schools found in raising money from external agencies

Lack of companies/industry in area; no SRB status
Form-filling and bureaucracy of the application process
Charitable trusts' criteria are difficult to satisfy and need expertise
Difficulty in raising matched funding
Bids are daunting
Too many bids to make; too much competition for them
Bid and similar funds do not always match the needs of the school
Intimidating process: too difficult
Not enough information on grant sources
Don't know criteria for success
Competition between schools; too many chasing too little
No success, unlucky, often turned down, discouraged
Need access and contacts to make it happen
Paperwork is over complex; form-filling bureaucracy

Information needs

In cases lack of up-to-date accurate information was seen as a difficulty. 87% of the secondary schools told us that they felt in need of further information and training, with 8% schools indicating either that they already knew or did not want to.

TABLE 9.2
Preferred form of information.

	No. of schools	% total sample
Information on fundraising sources	335	80
Training courses	144	34
Conferences	69	16

10 Secondary school fundraising for other causes

We wanted to find out where charity fundraising fitted in to the school's priorities. Many secondary schools are pioneering ambitious developments in citizenship education that encourage pupils to design and carry through their own community action programmes or to work closely with local organisations. Although it is widely feared that young people do not give to charities as much as their elders, school fundraising may have been overlooked.

The outlook is hopeful provided charities learn, as businesses have, to become active members of the school community, and to listen and contribute, not just ask. Table 10.1 is also reproduced in the primary school findings. It lists, in order of frequency of naming, the main comments made by schools about fundraising for other charities and community causes, and should give charity fundraisers some insight into how best to approach a school.

TABLE 10.1

Secondary schools' comments on fundraising for non-school charities

Too many requests received
Charities expect too much too often
Educational value is important
Keen on events (eg. Comic Relief; Children in Need)
Important to raise awareness of others
Very important/part of the school's ethos
Getting harder, only prepared to do joint fundraising: percentage for the school
Need to balance fundraising for school with needs of others
Need to balance local and national charities
Specific projects only, must be learning based or fun
Choose both local and national charities
Importance of local charities
Pupils' altruism is central
Choose local, national and international charities
Like topical charities, for curriculum input
Time consuming
Easier to fundraise for non-school charities than for school itself

TABLE 10.2

Secondary schools which raise money for activities for the benefit of the local community or for non-school charities.

	No. of schools	% total sample
Yes	373	89
No	17	4

TABLE 10.3

Amounts raised for charity and community causes in secondary schools

	Amounts raised £
Amount for local community:	728,144
Amount for other charities:	905,083
Total raised by responding schools:	1,633,227
Average for all secondary schools: (Assuming that the non-responding schools raised no funds for these purposes)	3,899

Total amount raised by secondary schools for others

An indicative national estimate, if these samples are assumed to be representative, is that:

• all secondary schools in England may be raising over £14 million a year for charities and local community causes (10% of the amount they raise for themselves), an impressive figure in view of the competing demands for their own needs.

FINDINGS

FUNDRAISING IN INDEPENDENT SCHOOLS IN ENGLAND

This supplementary survey of 90 independent schools in England was carried out in June–August 1999. All the schools provided for pupils over the ages of 11 or 13, i.e. were 'secondary' independent schools.

MAIN FINDINGS

How much independent schools raise

Of the independent schools responding over the year 1997–98:
- 25% chose not to supply this information.

Of those that did respond:
- 7% were raising less than £1,000, or no additional income;
- 70% were raising more than £10,000 a year; and
  of these:
  39% were raising more than £250,000 a year;
  22% were raising over £500,000 a year.

An indicative estimate of the amounts raised by all independent schools in England that provide secondary education can be made on the basis of these figures. Schools were not asked to display the precise amounts raised, but were asked to say into which of a number of bands their fundraising fell. On the assumption that the responding schools were representative and that, on average, their fundraised income lay at the middle of the band named, national figures as follows are indicated for independent secondary schools in England:

- £210 million a year (an average of around £249,000 per school) raised by independent schools in England from sources outside their fee income and main school budget. (A few may have regarded fee income as 'additional' income.)

It is important to note that this average is heavily influenced by the large sums raised by the estimated 39% of schools raising over £250,000. If these schools are excluded, the average per independent school in the remaining 61% drops to £31,400 per school. The much wider spread of income per school in this sector is evident, as is the much higher level of fundraised and other non-fee income available to a small number of highly influential schools.

- 32% of the schools surveyed said they had ongoing development appeals. Of these, 27 schools supplied us with information showing that, if taken together, the total long-term appeal target was £99,840,000, of which these 27 schools had, to date, raised in total £15,297,400. A very small number of well-known schools had set long-term appeal targets of £2 million, £10 million or even, in one case, £50 million. These are challenging ambitions, even in comparison with the appeals raised by large national charities.

Main sources of support for independent schools

- charitable trusts were the highest non-parental funders of independent schools, followed by companies;
- independent schools made less use of parental fundraising, partly because catchment areas were wider, with some pupils boarding, and because it was perceived to be unfair to invite parents who were already paying high fees to support future development. Alumni fundraising amongst ex-pupils was used extensively.

- non-teaching staff such as development managers and bursars provided fundraising and appeal support, taking much of the day-to-day burden off the shoulders of senior staff. This seems likely to make a difference to the organisation of fundraising.

Factors affecting independent school fundraising include:

- old stereotypes are not easily applied to the independent schools of today. Within the sector, the schools vary widely from the ancient public boarding and day schools to newly established proprietorial schools run for profit, small 'alternative' schools, or faith-linked schools with little income other than modest fees. Some, in particular the Muslim and other minority faith schools, would prefer to be maintained schools provided their ethos could be retained, and an increasing number are succeeding;

- the withdrawal of the assisted places scheme by the new Labour government has led many independent schools to fundraise for bursaries to assist pupils from lower income families;

- charitable trusts appear to provide a higher level of support for independent schools than for maintained sector schools:

- greater use is made by independent schools of tax-effective giving;

- 80% of English independent schools responding said they needed more information and training on sources and methods of fundraising;

- most assumed they were ineligible for the New Opportunities Fund and only 7% said they intended to apply.

Independent school fundraising for charitable and community causes

Of the independent schools responding:
- 86% said they raised money for charities and community causes;
- an average of around £7,300 per school was being raised by all independent schools surveyed. We counted the non-responding schools as raising zero income for others.

An indicative national estimate, if this sample is assumed to be representative, is that:

- independent schools in England, in total, may be raising over £6 million a year for charities and local community causes (i.e.giving overall only 3% of the amount they raise for themselves, although the highest average in the survey for the amounts raised per school).

HOW THE RESEARCH WAS CARRIED OUT

This small-scale survey of 90 independent secondary (11+ and 13+) schools in England was carried out by the Directory of Social Change in 1999–2000, alongside and as supplement to the surveys of mainstream primary and secondary schools. Our questionnaires, which were largely directed at maintained schools, were not specially adapted to the specific circumstances of the independent sector. This enabled us to make direct comparisons between sectors. However it also left much unexplored that deserves further investigation, notably the very wide range of schools now classified as 'independent', including small experimental schools, Muslim and other faith schools, day schools, boarding schools, the ancient public schools (and, according to DfEE statistics, the CTCs). The report also does not comment on the investment income received from endowments by some of the richer independent schools. In almost all cases the financial information shown applies to the year 1997–98.

Sample

In June 1999 questionnaires were sent out to 400 independent maintained secondary schools, alongside the secondary schools mailing.

Response rate

We received, in total, 90 replies: 23 % of the sample and approximately 11% of all independent secondary schools in England. It is not easy to know exactly how many secondary (11+ and 13+) independent secondary schools there are in England, since official (DfEE) statistics give only the total number of independent schools: 2,242, of which well over half must be preparatory schools. About half the independent schools are members of the Independent Schools Information Service (ISIS), but ISIS members also include preparatory schools. The figure we have used here (850) as an assumed total of all independent schools in England is an approximation drawn from published league tables, after excluding around 30 schools as likely to be 'crammer' coaching establishments rather than 'schools' in the sense of this survey.

Data

Where figures used in the tables below are not based on the total number of responding schools, the figure from which the table is derived ('the respondents') is stated. Where figures have been rounded, there may be minor discrepancies between the sum of the constituent parts and the totals as shown. Here, above all, caution should be exercised when drawing national conclusions: a high proportion of the schools chose not to disclose the amounts they raised, and the questionnaire did not investigate the return the richest schools receive from endowments and investments, in some cases by far their greatest source of non-fee income.

RESULTS

1 How much is raised by independent schools

The amounts raised by independent secondary schools in England with pupils over the age of 11 are spread more widely than those in any sectors covered by our survey. 25% of the schools surveyed provided no actual figures for their annual non-fee income. 7% of schools responding were raising less than £1,000 a year or nothing at all; 29% said they were raising not more than £10,000 a year. However, nearly 70% of the schools responding were raising over £10,000 a year, of which 26% were raising over £250,000.

The survey results, if representative of all independent schools in England, suggest that the total raised by independent schools is around £210 million a year, with a small number also setting high targets for longer-term development appeals. No questions about income from property and investments were included in the questionnaire; the major public schools that (to their credit) replied to our mailing were economical in drawing this omission to our attention.

TABLE 1
Financial support raised by independent schools in addition to the main school budget 1997–98.
Respondents: 67

	No. of schools	%
Less than £1,000	5	7
£1,001–£5,000	10	15
£5,001–£10,000	5	7
£10,001–£15,000	4	6
£15,001–£25,000	4	6
£25,001–£35,000	2	3
£35,001–£50,000	3	4
£50,001–£100,000	5	7
£100,001–250,000	3	4
£250,001–£500,000	11	16
Over £500,000	15	22

2 What independent schools raise money for

Computers topped the list of independent school needs, followed closely, as elsewhere, by funding for school building, books, sports and music. Independent schools without endowments to support their buildings must raise new capital expenditure over several years, since fees cannot be varied to take account of capital expenditure. We were surprised to find independent schools seeking to raise money for stationery and teachers' salaries: both items were named by the same school, which alleged funder prejudice against the independent sector but was also keen to receive advice on fundraising.

TABLE 2
What independent schools raise money for

Items	Independent schools naming	% total sample (90)
Computers	37	41
School buildings	30	33
Library	27	30
Sports/music tours	27	30
Music equipment	23	26
Sports equipment	23	26
Books	20	22
Playground	17	19
Trips	15	17
Minibuses	11	12
Furniture	9	10
School grounds	7	8
Swimming pool	7	8
Gym	5	6
Specialist arts help	3	3
Parents' facilities	2	2
Stationery	1	1
Teachers' salaries	1	1

3 How independent schools raise money

Although some independent schools, like maintained sector schools, still appeared to rely heavily on events, typically the independent sector used a more sophisticated approach and a wider range of fundraising methods.

49% of independent schools were engaged in trading activities (such as the letting of the school for conference purposes, or providing sports and other facilities at a charge). 11% said this was their most successful venture. Most striking was the greater use made by the independent schools of tax-effective means of giving, with, for example, 56% of the sample inviting covenants and 41% benefiting from legacy income. Gift Aid is likely to increase as new fiscal regimes make it easier to donate small amounts tax-effectively without the long-term commitment of a covenant.

TABLE 3.1
The most frequently reported fundraising methods in independent schools

	No. of schools	% total sample
Events	61	68
Trading	44	49
Sponsorship	15	17
200 Clubs	10	11
Affinity cards	1	1
Tax-effective giving		
Covenants	50	56
Gift Aid	40	44
Legacies	37	41

Development Appeals

Far more independent schools (33% of those responding, compared with about 21% of maintained secondary schools and 8% of primary schools) had established a development appeal.

There were various objects of these development appeals. We show details of 27 of them in Table 3.3, noting the frequent mentions of bursary appeals for pupils from families unable to pay full fees; that nearly 25% of the independent schools were using their appeal for sports facilities; and that several schools presented their appeals as for facilities that could also be used by the community, though usually out of school hours and for a fee.

These are major appeals, even by the standards of large charities, and it will be interesting to see how they fare.

TABLE 3.2

Independent schools with development appeals.
Respondents: 89

	No. of schools	%
Yes	29	33
No	60	67

TABLE 3.3

No. of independent schools with development appeals: by purpose, target and amounts raised

Purpose of the appeal	Target £	Amount raised to date £
Barn conversion	150,000	50,000
Buildings	3,000,000	no figure given
Bursary appeal	2,000,000	410,000
Bursaries/new facilities/computers	4,000,000	150,000
Endowment/bursaries	20,000,000	2,000,000
Endowment/ bursaries scheme	500,000	no figure given
IT facilities and library	60,000	32,000
Long-term/endowment/development	50,000,000	4,000,000
Long-term/endowment/scholarships /development	10,000,000	3,000,000
New buildings	100,000	72,000
Needs of an ongoing nature	no figure given	
Open-ended: a rolling list	no figure given	150,000
Performing arts	2,000,000	no figure given
Scholarships	100,000	no figure given
School hall: renew	50,000	3,000
School hall: new	400,000	386,000
Science block	1,100,000	604,000
Science labs: refurbish	20,000	6,000
Sports complex for national, local and school use	2,000,000	750,000
Sports facilities	500,000	385,000
Sports facilities	600,000	300,000
Sport hall	400,000	200,000
Sports hall	750,000	30,000
Sports hall	2,000,000	no figure given
School hall: renew	50,000	3,000
Swimming pool	35,000	9,400
Theatre	75,000	60,000
Total	**99,890,000**	**12,600,400**

4 How fundraising is managed in independent schools

We wanted to know two things: who organised the fundraising in schools and who held, controlled (and so was accountable for) the funds themselves. This was an issue familiar to the independent schools, where around half are constituted as not-for-profit charities, and where it is customary to employ a bursar who is likely to be aware of the advantages and obligations of charitable status.

Who organises the work

In the independent sector, the headteachers were still at the top of the list, though it was interesting to note that the teachers in the independent sector were less directly involved than their counterparts in the maintained sector. Their governors, on the other hand, were more actively involved.

Development officer, resource manager, fundraiser, fundraising consultant

One reason for the lightened management burden on teaching staff was that the independent schools could afford to employ professional non-teaching assistance with fundraising. The development officer (where development is the politically sound term for fundraising) feature in 19% of independent schools, compared with only 2% in the maintained sector. Resource managers are also more common as are external fundraisers.

TABLE 4.1
Persons named as having prime responsibility for independent school fundraising.
Respondents: 75

	No. of schools	%	% (cf maintained sec. schools)
Headteacher	25	33	48
Deputy head	1	1	13
Department head	1	1	3
Governors	7	9	2
Parents	14	19	27
Development officer	14	19	2
Resource manager	8	11	6
External fundraiser	5	15	6

Who holds the funds

Table 4.2 tests the general awareness of charity law within the schools and amongst their supporters, including the fact that small charities in England and Wales raising £1,000 or more a year are now required to register with the Charity Commission. For the independent sector the regulatory requirements, if not easier, are at least more clear-cut than in the evolving charitable sector within the state system.

TABLE 4.2
Funds contributing to and holding independent school fundraising income

	Fund contributes financially		Fund is a registered charity	
	No. schools	% total sample (55)	No. of schools	Col. 3 as % of col. 1
HSA/PTA	44	49	12	27
Friends' Association	41	46	17	41
Prize Funds	46	51	22	48
Department funds	12	13	1	8
Fundraising Committee	20	22	5	25
Endowment Fund	25	28	17	68
Trust Funds	23	26	16	70

5 Main sources of support for independent schools

Parents and friends

Few independent schools had Parent–Teacher Associations, Home–School Associations or Friends' Associations, and if they had, only a small number (eight schools) reported seeing them as their main source of non-fee income. This was probably because they were more likely to have development appeals run by committees of distinguished local people or old pupils, though often with some parental participation.

The bid culture, companies and trusts

Independent schools obviously did not have the same access as maintained schools to local authority bid funds, but some had benefited from European funds of various kinds, usually for language exchanges.

Charitable trusts

The fact that charitable trusts were named by 42% of responding independent schools is striking in comparison with only 23% of maintained secondary schools. This is partly explained by the reluctance of some charitable trusts (often with the best of motives) to fund 'those things which it is the duty of the state to provide'. However, it is also likely that many charity trustees were educated in the independent sector and see it as a worthy beneficiary of trust funding; some major contributions also come from family trusts with personal links to particular schools. It is also the case that some charitable trusts are explicitly concerned with funding independent schools, either with capital support or extensive bursary and scholarship schemes.

Companies

Companies, on the other hand, were cited as financial supporters by only 19% of independent schools as major funders, compared with 34% of secondary schools. Companies wish to add value to the major players in any market, and no doubt see the maintained sector, which will supply most of their future workforce, in this light. Some of the largest have well thought-out programmes of corporate citizenship designed to benefit as wide a range of pupils as possible, including the provision of curriculum materials, the best of which are excellent.

It is, however, worth observing that company sponsorship is a different class of giving, designed to promote the company as much if not more than the school; hence VAT is payable on such transactions. Some major public schools, notably Eton, have received considerable sponsorship from companies, often foreign investors, whose motives are not, and not required to be, altruistic.

Trading

Another feature of the independent schools' approach to fundraising is the emphasis on income generation of all kinds, backed by the accounting systems to handle it. Some maintained secondary schools are now learning from this example and trading on a scale beyond the teatowel. Some independent schools were investing in, or seeking funding for, facilities that could be hired out to the public for community use: a fine-sounding proposition, often also genuinely intended to be a local benefit, but usually also a way to add to income. The long experience of some independent school bursars pays dividends here; estate and premises management for largescale profit is not a task for fledgling fundraisers and requires considerable management expertise, not to mention time.

TABLE 5.1

External funders supporting independent schools

Frequency of naming	Financial support	Gifts in kind
Charitable trusts	38	1
Companies	17	6
European Funds	5	0
TECs	2	0
Arts Council	2	0
Sports Council	2	1
European Funds	2	0
Diocesan Funds	1	0
Community Chest	0	1

We have omitted from this table the various government and local authority grants, such as SRB and City Challenge funds, which do not apply to the independent sector.

6 The impact of the National Lottery on independent schools

The first five 'good causes'

Of the five original 'good causes' of the National Lottery, enterprising schools with match funding from their local authority or other partners could use the system to get major awards for arts or sports facilities primarily for community use but also available to pupils in school hours. Of the total independent school sample, three headteachers said that their schools had already benefited from the various National Lottery Funds: two from the Sports fund and one from the Arts fund. The comparable figures for the secondary school sample (four times as large) were 43 for Sports and 15 for Arts.

The New Opportunities Fund (NOF): the sixth good cause

Very few independent schools intended to apply for NOF funding. Many felt their applications would take a low priority over others. Unlike the other sectors in our survey, it was noticeable that many of those who were satisfied with the information received had deliberately chosen not to apply. It appears that the NOF has already a reputation for funding the most needy first – an expectation which should be fulfilled.

TABLE 6

Independent schools intending to apply for the New Opportunities Fund.

	No. of schools	% total sample (90)
Yes	6	7
No	62	69

Satisfaction with information supplied about the New Opportunities Fund

Base	No. of schools	%
Sufficient	23	26
Insufficient	55	61

7 Factors affecting independent school fundraising

Type and category of school

Not all independent schools are wealthy. Girls' schools are traditionally less well-funded than boys' schools, and day schools are generally, but not always, less well-funded than the boarding schools. Some 'alternative' independent schools are established with little money by those who want a less centrally controlled and examination-led education system for their children; other schools are set up by those who would much prefer to be part of the state system, if they could obtain state funding for a school reflecting, for example, their Muslim religious ethos.

Most of the schools can, however, draw on a much better-off circle of potential donors. It clearly helps to have parents who can afford school fees, but this is also a constraint. Schools reported that they felt unable to ask current parents to support endowment appeals for future generations at the same time as they were paying fees. Alumni fundraising, targeted at old pupils and staff, was an alternative exploited more readily in the independent sector than elsewhere, perhaps for obvious reasons.

The recent withdrawal of the assisted places scheme, whereby government contributed to the fees of selected children whose families could not afford them in full, has been a major recent influence on the funding objectives of independent schools seeking bursaries to replace it.

8 Disadvantage, deprivation and independent school fundraising

A common perception is that independent schools cater on the whole for the better-off families; this is countered by the insistence of many of the schools that they benefit poor and needy children, usually of high ability, through the scholarships and bursaries offered to assist them.

Only two of the independent schools surveyed (2%) had more than 10% of pupils receiving free school meals. 25 of the independent schools responding (30%) said that they had some pupils with free school meals. A number of these schools had previously been Direct Grant schools providing large numbers of able children with 'free places'.

We do not doubt the motives of the many schools that told us they were trying to raise funding to replace the assisted places scheme withdrawn by the incoming Labour government. However, their level of deprivation is relative.

9 Difficulties and information needs of independent schools

We asked schools for their further comments on fundraising problems and needs, and whether there were any local problems. 39 independent schools (68%) said they had difficulties in fundraising. Some showed themselves highly experienced fundraisers, others less so. Their complaints about form-filling echoed those of the maintained sector. A common complaint was that independent schools stood less chance than maintained sector schools of gaining company or trust funding: the second at least appears unlikely from the results here. A problem particular to independent schools was reluctance to approach parents, who felt they had already paid high fees.

Information needs

70 independent schools (80%) said they would like more information and training on fundraising.

10 Independent school fundraising for other causes

Independent schools were involved in charity fundraising but noticeably slower to support local community causes; most of their donations went to national charities. The schools were asked to place a figure on the total amount they had raised in 1997–98 for the community, and then for non-school charities.

TABLE 10.1
Independent schools raising money for charities and local community causes

	No. of schools	% total sample (90)
Yes	78	87
No	10	11

TABLE 10.2
Amounts raised by independent schools for charitable and community causes: 1997–98

	amounts raised £
Amount for local community:	191,123
Amount for other charities:	466,608
Total raised by responding schools	657,731
Average for all independent schools: (Assuming that the non-responding schools raised no funds for these purposes)	7,308

Total amount raised by independent schools for others

An indicative national estimate, if these samples are assumed to be representative, is that:

- independent schools in England, in total, may be raising over £6 million a year for charities and local community causes (i.e. giving 3% of the amount they raise for themselves, although the highest average in the survey for the amounts raised per school).

FINDINGS

FUNDRAISING IN SPECIAL SCHOOLS IN ENGLAND

This supplementary survey of 55 maintained and non-maintained special schools in England was carried out in June–August 1999.

MAIN FINDINGS

How much special schools raise

Of the special schools responding, over the year 1997–98:
- 21% were raising less than £1,000 a year, or no additional income;
- 26% were raising more than £10,000 a years
- 8% were raising more than £25,000 a year;

of which
- 2% were raising more than £50,000–£100,000;
- no special schools responding raised more than £100,000 a year;
- the highest proportion of special schools (42%) raised between £1,000–£5,000 a year.

An indicative estimate of the amounts raised by all special schools in England (excluding independent special schools) can be made on the basis of these figures. Schools were not asked to display the precise amount raised, but to say into which of a number of bands their fundraising fell. On the assumption that the responding schools were representative, and that, on average, their fundraised income lay at the middle of the band named, this may appear at first sight to indicate a national figure as follows:
- £10.5 million a year (an average of £8,500 a school or £110 per pupil) raised by English special schools from sources outside their mainstream school budget. However, this average is heavily influenced by the large sums raised by the 8% of schools raising over £25,000 a year. The high per pupil average income is also influenced by the much smaller pupil numbers and the high cost of special teaching equipment.

Main sources of support for special schools
- schools for physically disabled pupils gained more fundraising help than other types of school from local voluntary organisations and clubs such as Lions and Rotary, services such as police, armed services and firefighters, or local shops and pubs;
- this compensated in part for the fact that school catchment areas were wide, some schools were residential, and parents often lived too far away to help out on a regular basis; some however, remained highly active supporters;
- although company support was very difficult to attract, sports and social clubs attached to local companies were often anxious to help;
- 47% of special schools were intending to apply to the New Opportunities Fund.

Factors affecting special school fundraising include:
- the low pupil numbers;
- the wide catchment areas;
- the specialist educational needs of pupils for special equipment to enable their learning;

- the need to liaise closely and appropriately with external supporters;
- the schools' limited sponsorship appeal for local employers;
- a particular problem that special school teachers identified was the fine line to tread between thanking supporters, publicising support, and embarrassing their physically disabled pupils by unnecessary exposure to well-intentioned but ill-focused pity;
- schools where pupils were emotionally or behaviourally disturbed faced a different problem: their pupils were far less attractive to public funders, and their special programmes often had very high costs;
- 66% of special schools responding said they needed more information and training on sources and methods of fundraising;
- 44% of special schools responding said they had insufficient information about the New Opportunities Fund.

Special school fundraising for charitable and community causes

Of the special schools responding:
- 61% said they raised money for charities and community causes;
- an average of £430 a school was being raised by all special schools surveyed. (We counted the non-responding schools as raising zero income for others.)

An indicative national estimate, if this sample is assumed to be representative, is that:
- in total, special schools in England may be raising £0.5 million a year for charities and local community causes (3% of the amount they raise for themselves).

HOW THE RESEARCH WAS CARRIED OUT

This small-scale survey of maintained and non-maintained special schools in England was carried out by the Directory of Social Change in 1999–2000, alongside and as a supplement to the surveys of mainstream primary and secondary schools. The questionnaires were not specially adapted to the specific circumstances of the special schools. In almost all cases financial information applies to the year 1997–98.

Sample

In June 1999 questionnaires were sent out to 195 special schools covering a range of special needs, i.e. about 16% of the 1,229 maintained and non-maintained special schools in England. The age ranges differ dramatically and the high numbers of all-age schools made it inappropriate to deal with them within the primary and secondary surveys. This was one reason for our decision to report separately on the special schools.

Response rate

We received, in total, 55 replies (28% of the sample, representing about 4% of all special schools in England), often from headteachers with strong views to express. Although the percentage response is high, the findings are based on a relatively small number of schools, so national estimates should be treated with caution.

Data

Where figures used in the Tables below are not based on the total figure from which the Table is derived responding schools, the figure from which the Table is derived ('the respondents') is stated. Where figures have been rounded, there may be minor discrepancies between the sum of the constituent parts and the totals as shown.

Note:
Maintained special schools are run by local education authorities, who pay all the expenses of maintenance.

Non-maintained special schools are run by voluntary bodies; they may receive some grant from the DfEE for capital work and for equipment, but their current expenditure is met primarily from fees charged to the local education authorities for pupils placed in the schools.

Independent fee-charging schools that provide wholly or mainly for pupils with special needs are not included in this survey.

RESULTS

1 How much is raised by special schools

The amounts raised by special schools in England differ greatly, at least in part as a reflection of the schools' own wide variations in pupil numbers, age-range and needs, and the specialism and category of the school itself, including whether or not it had a boarding unit. 60% of the special schools responding reported raising under £5,000 a year. Of these, 20% were raising less than £1,000. Only 1 school (2%) of the special schools surveyed was raising over £100,000 a year.

Table 1, if representative of all maintained and non-maintained special schools in England, suggests that the total raised by special schools is around £7 million a year, with a small number also setting high targets for longer-term development appeals.

Whilst all schools shared a view that fundraising was difficult, with low expectations of success, some schools, and special schools in particular, felt that raising the profile of the school was the primary aim of fundraising activities. Raising money was secondary to the need to make more people aware of the school, and to help give identity to the school community, in particular drawing attention not only to the needs of pupils but to their potential. Special schools were often very focused on this distinction, which is an important point for all schools to note.

TABLE 1

Financial support raised by special schools in addition to the main school budget 1997–98. Respondents: 53

	No. of schools	%
Less than £1,000	11	21
£1,001–£5,000	22	42
£5,001–£10,000	6	11
£10,001–£15,000	7	13
£15,001–£25,000	3	5
£25,001–£35,000	1	2
£35,001–£50,000	2	4
£50,001–£100,000	1	2
£100,001–250,000	0	0
£250,001–£500,000	0	0
More than £500,000	0	0

2 What special schools raise money for

Special schools raise money to supplement their local authority income in much the same way as other schools, although their priorities are not always quite the same as those of their colleagues in mainstream secondary schools. Minibuses, outdoor space and visits scored higher than elsewhere, but then came the familiar demand for IT and books. We also gave headteachers the opportunity to name other items for which funds are raised. As well as the items listed, the special schools were often raising money for specialist classroom equipment and multi–sensory aids. One school was raising support for a counselling service for parents, an innovative idea that deserves success. Most schools were raising money for more than one item or activity. 26 schools had raised support for between three and five activities, although 2 schools had raised money for 12 items, and one school for 13.

TABLE 2.1

What special schools raise money for

Items	No. of schools naming	% total sample (55)
Trips	38	69
Playground	27	49
Minibuses	25	45
Books	21	38
Computers	21	38
School grounds	17	31
Music equipment	17	31
Sports equipment	17	31
Library	12	22
Furniture	10	18
School buildings	6	11
Sports/music tours	6	11
Swimming pool	4	7
Specialist arts help	4	7
Swimming pool	4	7
Gym	3	5
Parents' facilities	1	2
Stationery	1	2
Teachers' salaries	0	0

3 How special schools raise money

We asked which of eight likely approaches to fundraising had been employed.

Special schools, like all schools, appeared still to rely heavily on events; unlike other special schools, however, they frequently have events organised on their behalf by others. The support of local fundraisers and charities was gratefully noted by several schools.

22% of special schools were engaged in trading activities and sponsorship was quite widely used. A small number were experimenting with 'affinity' credit cards, though as yet with little evidence of success. Little use was made of covenanting, compared with secondary schools.

TABLE 3.1

The most frequently reported fundraising methods in special schools

	No. of schools naming	% total sample (55)
Events	38	69
Sponsorship	13	24
Trading	12	22
200 Clubs	9	16
Affinity cards	0	0
None of these	6	11
Tax-effective giving		
Covenants	3	5
Gift Aid	3	5
Legacies	5	9

Development Appeals

We took the existence, or not, of a Development Appeal as another indicator of the sophistication of a school's fundraising approach. 9 special schools (21%) had established a development appeal, compared with about 20% of secondary schools and 8% of primary schools. Most special school appeals were for minibuses: in this sector pupil transport is surely an essential?

TABLE 3.3
Frequently named objects of development appeals in special schools

Purpose of the appeal	Target £	Amount raised to date £
Specialist toilet facilities	10,000	10,000
Minibus	10,000	2,000
Replace school bus	25,000	17,000
Multisensory room	10,000	7,000
Minibus	25,000	5,000
Lease contract for minibus	35,000	5,000
Multi-sensory environment	30,000	2,500
New bus	20,000	2,000
Overnight residential accommodation	15,000	1,700

4 How fundraising is managed in special schools

We wanted to know two things: who organised the fundraising in schools and who held, controlled (and so was accountable for) the funds themselves.

Who organises the work

Headteachers and other senior members of staff were highly scored by the special schools, with parents lower down the list. Here, too, governors were infrequently mentioned as fundraisers.

Unlike the primary schools, the special schools regularly named the deputy heads as leaders in fundraising. Some, but surprisingly few, of these respondents pointed out that the responsibility was shared.

TABLE 4.1
Persons named as having responsibility for special school fundraising

	No. of schools
Headteacher	28
Deputy head	4
Department head	3
Governors	3
Parents	12
Development officer	1
Resource manager	0
External fundraiser	0

Development officer, resource manager, fundraiser, fundraising consultant

Only one school said that it had a development officer in post.

Who holds the funds

Table 4.2 tests the general awareness of charity law within the schools and amongst their supporters, including the fact that small charities in England and Wales raising £1,000 or more a year are now required to register with the Charity Commission. The regulatory and accountability issues that arise from this little understood link between English schools and the Charity Commission are discussed at greater length elsewhere in the report.

TABLE 4.2

Funds contributing to and holding special school fundraising income

	Fund contributes financially		Fund is a registered charity	
	No. of schools	% total sample (55)	No. of schools	% of col. I (reported organisations of this type)
HSA–PTA	20	36	13	65
Friends' Association	26	47	13	50
Department Funds	11	20	0	20
Prize Funds	1	2	0	0
Fundraising Committee	14	25	3	21
Trust Funds	3	5	2	66
Endowment Fund	0	0	0	0

5 Main sources of support for special schools

Parents and friends

Although parents were willing, they already had many problems to cope with, and often lived some distance from the school, so natural networks did not grow up as easily as in other sectors covered by this survey. Despite their personal responsibilities, often including struggles to raise funding for equipment needed by their own children, many special school parents did take part in school fundraising.

Even where no formal Friends' Association existed, the special schools sometimes found it easier to obtain support from their local community. Schools specialising in the care of physically disabled children often became the target of fundraising efforts by local charities and social clubs, and welcomed these additional forms of income, although they were seldom high amounts.

TABLE 5.1

Special schools naming HSAs/PTAs or Friends' Associations as their main supporters
Respondents: 35

	No. of schools	% total sample (55)	naming as main source
Home–School or Parent–Teacher Association		18	33
Friends' Association		17	22
Total		35	55

The bid culture, companies and trusts

60% of the special schools felt that there were difficulties in raising money from non-LEA funders. These difficulties were in part similar to those experienced by colleagues in mainstream schools. Information was not easily available, the amount of time needed was prohibitive and the competition between schools and other organisations were all demotivating. Generally it was felt that funding criteria are not friendly towards special schools, particularly where a project (such as toilet facilities) is not attractive to fund. (The GEST/Standards Fund is excluded here, since it is virtually an aspect of mainstream funding, although many schools reminded us of its significance in their budgets.)

The size of the school was often a particular obstacle, in terms of the personnel to put applications together, the number of beneficiaries that would be helped and the smaller parental and community support that could be expected. One school reported that it had applied to 50 charitable trusts and had received only one reply; £500 had been raised to date.

TABLE 5.2
External funders supporting special schools

Frequency of naming	Financial support	Gifts in kind	% (col 1 as % total sample 55)
Charitable trusts	17	1	31
Companies	17	5	31
Education Business Partnerships	11	0	20
TECs	7	1	13
Single Regeneration Budget (SRB)	7	0	13
Arts Council	6	0	11
Sports Council	3	1	5
European Funds	2	0	4
Diocesan Funds	1	0	2
Community Chest	1	0	
Safer Cities	1	0	2
City Challenge	0	0	
Department of Health	0	0	0
Task Force	0	0	0
Urban Development Corporation	0	0	0
None of these	3	5	9

6 The impact of the National Lottery on special schools

The first five 'good causes'

Of the five original 'good causes' of the National Lottery, enterprising schools with match funding from their local authority or other partners could use the system to get major awards for arts or sports facilities primarily for community use but also available to pupils in school hours. Of the total special school sample, only two said that their schools had already benefited from the various National Lottery Funds, both from the Arts Fund.

The New Opportunities Fund (NOF): the sixth good cause

If the percentage in Table 5.2 is typical of the country as a whole, special schools stand a high chance of success when applying for NOF funds – the odds are worth the effort of application. A significant proportion of those who did not plan to apply or who were undecided said they had received insufficient information to make a firm judgement.

TABLE 6
Special schools intending to apply for the New Opportunities Fund.

	No. of schools	% total sample (55)
Yes	26	47
No	23	42

Satisfaction with information supplied about the New Opportunities Fund

	No. of schools	%
Sufficient	29	53
Insufficient	24	44

Non-maintained special schools, which are independent special schools run by voluntary bodies, often with residential accommodation, need to raise their own funds for capital buildings and major development. Their fee-payers, almost entirely local authorities not individual parents, do not provide a donor base to support such work.

Special schools stressed that having a wide catchment area, or being a small school with a particular intake, often prevented them from taking advantage of fundraising opportunities.

7 Disadvantage, deprivation and special school fundraising

Many special schools were well aware of the nature of disadvantage and the stereotyping to which their own variety of disadvantage could give rise. Some schools felt that the prime purpose of their fundraising was the raise the profile of the school, to make people more aware of its pupils and to help give identity to the school community, which makes them useful role models for others dealing with different forms of disadvantage.

As with other schools, special schools in areas of deprivation find it hard to raise money, a double disadvantage. The following tables use the proportion of pupils receiving free school meals as an indicator of disadvantage. There did not appear to be any relationship between the amounts raised in special schools and the percentage of pupils in the school in receipt of free school meals.

TABLE 7.
Numbers of special schools with pupils in receipt of free school meals.
Respondents: 55

	No. of schools	%
None	1	2
less than 10% receive free meals	3	5
10%–25% receive free meals	12	22
25%–50% receive free meals	19	35
50%–75% receive free meals	16	29
75%–100% receive free meals	3	5

8 Difficulties and information needs of special schools

We asked respondents for their further comments on their school's fundraising, and whether there were any local problems or notable opportunities. The problem of client groups that did not command much 'sympathy' or interest was frequently aired. The small numbers of pupils in the school made it difficult for the schools to engage in generating funds through voucher sponsorships and so on. 33 schools (60%) said they had difficulties in fundraising.

TABLE 8.
Special schools wishing to receive more fundraising information

	No. of schools	% total sample (55)
Yes	47	85
No	7	13

Preferred form of information

	No. of schools	% sample
Information on fundraising sources	46	84
Training courses	23	42
Conferences	11	20

9 Special school fundraising for other causes

Sections on primary and secondary schools have noted the remarkable extent to which – often despite their own needs – schools were raising substantial sums for other charitable and community causes. It is perhaps even more remarkable that the special schools too are raising substantial amounts for these purposes.

TABLE 9.1
Special schools which raise money for activities for the benefit of the local community or for non-school charities. Respondents: 55

	No. of schools	% sample (55)
Yes	34	62
No	19	35

TABLE 9.2
Amounts raised for charity and community causes in special schools

	Amounts raised £
Amount for local community:	9,805
Amount for other charities:	13,789
Total raised by responding schools:	23,594
Average for all special schools: (Assuming that the non-responding schools raised no funds for these purposes)	430

Total amount raised by special schools for others

An indicative national estimate, if these samples are assumed to be representative, is that:

- in total, special schools in England may be raising £0.5 million a year for charities and local community causes (or 5% of the amount they raise for themselves), an impressive total.

WHAT THE TEACHERS SAID

About school fundraising in general

"This is not the purpose for which teachers are employed."

"We are at an early stage of developing a fundraising strategy. We realise that we need to build long-term relationships with our community and then see what opportunities they bring."

"Fundraising has community benefit, but involves massive effort. Social rewards, rather than financial benefits, tend to be the main outcome here. The notion of schools as 'community regenerators' is the most powerful one we have come across so far – with benefits for both school and community."

"Fundraising is an essential part of life in modern schools."

"It can be very time-consuming, whether organising events, building and maintaining networks, seeking external agency support or completing the necessary submissions."

"In our experience, fundraising in the inner city is a nightmare."

"I feel that all schools should be funded sufficiently and that there should be no need for fundraising. All our energies should go into teaching the children."

"It would be interesting to know how much funding is raised by parents to support the educational system. Budget shares, particularly in small schools, are run on a very fine margin, and even small fundraising events can have significant consequences."

"Colleagues from Finland and France regard this aspect of our work as totally unacceptable. I can't say I disagree, but in Britain we simply accept it as part of school life."

"We're pretty good at it – there's a fee payable if you want to learn more!"

"The opportunities are all around us, but the time is not."

About the purposes for which schools raise money

"The key is to take things you planned to do and see if you can obtain support to enhance them. It would not be such a good idea just to react to funding opportunities, and change what you intended to do in order to obtain the money."

"We are a small rural community with a big heart. We are always fundraising (just like everyone else) to provide 'extras' the budget in the school, or in the county, can't afford. We are in competition with others, whilst trying not to interfere with other excellent causes. This is a problem. Resources and goodwill will only stretch so far. We work very hard, sometimes for very little, but each bit helps towards our vision of providing better facilities for our children."

"As 90% of school budgets go towards salaries, trying to buy resources or maintain things, with costs rising, is becoming worse and worse every year."

"We are under pressure to consider fundraising to provide basic equipment and materials. We prefer to keep fundraising for 'special' events and charitable reasons. Underfunding in mainstream activities, such as staffing, undermines the benefits schools can derive from fundraising. Pressure to raise funds detracts from the other educational issues that must be addressed."

"We are a tiny school, receiving tremendous support from the parents (27 families) and the community, but we are too small to qualify for additional funding for capital works via the local education authority. We desperately need more space to accommodate the needs of the 21st century curriculum in a 19th [century] building. We have had to explore the possible future use of the premises in this remote rural community, involving other groups in order to cross the divide between education funding and community funding."

"Since October 1998 we have embarked upon a huge project to raise £120,000 to replace two classroom huts with permanent purpose-built classrooms attached to the main building. A charitable trust has been set up and £45,000 has been raised so far, mostly deeds of covenant, with many people in the village supporting the project. We were unsuccessful in our bid to DfEE and our LEA has been unable to allocate any capital funds. £120,000 is a huge target for any small school and village."

About the bid culture

"Money should be distributed more equitably — it should not just go to those who prioritse the process of bidding, rather than putting teaching and learning first."

"We can't afford to have a dedicated role for someone to write bids."

"Some applications are too elaborate and complex in their format, resulting (assuming we are not alone) in many being unsuccessful."

"Much of the TEC money is not directed at 11–16 schools in any meaningful longterm way."

"[Fundraising] diverts staff from the main focus of educational activity. As government is now becoming data-rich about schools, a pro rata division of monies [according to need] should be possible. Alternatively, bidding for funds should be taken over by the LEAs, not individual institutions."

"We depend on SRB and NOF."

"The bidding culture is a nightmare. There is no doubt, however, that funding obtained in this way can be used to lever other funds. We have found that, e.g. SRB funding can help us to lever funding, and we have had some significant success at this."

"Serious fundraising to support specific school development needs proper planning and time. I'm a class-based headmaster, with only 7–10 in each class. I would be delighted if consortium planning or partnership bidding could be arranged. Many of my colleagues in neighbouring small schools are in the same position. We need funds but are unable to plan specific bids. Coordinated bids across a group of schools, led by a 'bid manager', would help me and my colleagues. My secondary 'link' school is helping us do some of this work."

About charitable trusts

"At present education can't fund us, and many charities won't – because it is perceived to be an 'education' problem!"

"Charitable trusts seem to have more requirements than resources."

"We have contacted every charitable trust we feel has an educational slant, without success."

"Many charitable trusts do not want to support schools because they believe most things should be covered by statutory funding."

"When we had a specific appeal three years ago, to raise funds for our drama studio and library, we employed a fundraiser who put us on to a multitude of charitable trusts. The only ones who responded were local ones with which we have contacts, all the rest turned us down, which put us off the whole idea. Local charities support us. No national ones to date have done so."

"Schools should be funded according to their needs. Obviously this isn't going to happen, and so the application for funding from charitable trusts becomes a necessity. However, it takes so much time to apply. We had a small grant from the Sports and Arts Foundation. On several occasions after we applied, a letter came back from the foundation, doing all they could to put us off having the application go through to the next and subsequent stages, e.g. 'Obviously we (the foundation) have more applications than funds, so if you wish to withdraw at this stage we would understand' ... that's the gist of it. I kept writing back and saying that I wanted to proceed. Why else would I apply in the first place? And why should I have to keep having to make a reply to a ridiculous request."

About companies

"We are in a perceived socially deprived area, with a majority of low attaining pupils. Businesses seem to want to be associated only with 'better' schools."

"The local companies support us all, and various initiatives, e.g. Safeways vouchers for transport, are of great benefit."

"We used to have several local businesses who supported us. Unfortunately many of these have closed down. However, we have found out that by raising our own profile, we are getting more local support. It is hard work and a time-consuming process."

"Local companies have been approached on numerous occasions, but they are unwilling to commit even moderate sums, whereas schools in the suburbs have attracted large sums from rail companies, motor manufacturers and insurance companies."

"We have good links with a number of local companies that support our awards evening with prizes of money and goods, and support us with work experience and personnel support to our students. We have been successful in gaining sponsorship from an international company for a summer literacy school."

About the New Opportunities Fund

"We are in a very poor area and it is difficult to raise money. I am really disgusted at the response of the NOF: the letter they sent me was very bland, offered no real reason for turning us down. Also, the form was very difficult to understand. I was given help through the Early Years Service and they thought we were a deserving case and stood a very good chance of funding."

About fundraising difficulties

"We have few rich or influential parents or governors, no rich and prosperous local companies, and all the money that comes from local or national government has 'strings' attached."

"We have serious difficulties in raising funds, even though we have a lot of needs. Our main problems are lack of time and expertise."

"In our school we have so few teachers that this aspect causes even more difficulties, as we are so pressed for time. Also our local community is not well off, and can become disaffected by too much pressure for funding."

"We live and work in a relatively poor area. We are always asking the same families for the money. There is no time to read all the information regarding other ways of raising money, or to fill in forms."

"Our biggest problem is time-labour. We are only a small village and funds are easily exhausted; there's a large comprehensive close by that is also appealing to the same small community."

"Schools big enough to employ professional fundraisers are advantaged."

"Primary schools are under-funded even more noticeably than secondary schools. As all staff have full teaching timetables, there is never anyone who can organise or administer this aspect of school life. Business and commerce often see a payback in supporting secondary schools but small rural primary schools like this are very disadvantaged. Parents in the area earn, on average, 25% less than the average English wage. Therefore even the PTA struggles to raise money."

"Fundraising activities are minimally successful in urban disadvantaged areas."

About parents

"Parental expectation is that government should pay for all educational needs. They resent being approached for any voluntary contribution, and always want something in it for them: a course, a concert or party, or the chance of a prize."

"Parents in inner city areas tend not to be from the professional groups, and therefore their fundraising potential is limited."

"This is a poor area and parents have little extra money. It is difficult to find parents who are willing to give up their time to organise events."

About being an independent school

"The school and its catchment area does not attract funds from government or local authority sources, although we have competed for a number of projects. This may be due to our independence, but we tend to feel that we do not appear to have difficulties as a school, academically or socially. We are never given priority for funding. We are a very popular school, our classes are increasing and we need more space to offer the quality teaching and learning that already exists in the school."

"Our problem is that, quite naturally, when we are competing for funds locally, anybody not linked to us will tend to donate funds towards the maintained sector rather than to us, an independent school. Advice on how to tackle this particular problem would be appreciated."

"Funds are raised from fee income although we have the benefit of charitable trust status."

"We do very little fundraising as we're owned by a profit-making company."

"The perceived current antipathy by government to independent education makes it difficult for organisations to be seen to help develop this educational sector. Part of this school is a scheduled ancient monument with a number of 12th century buildings. We were unable to obtain help from English Heritage for recent essential maintenance for these buildings."

"Independent schools often have charitable status because many of them perform charitable activities themselves. The contribute to the local community and provide facilities for the local community. We have charitable status. We also have a voluntary service group which actively goes out into the community to help the under-privileged. The daughters of supposedly 'rich' parents are going out and learning about voluntary services. However, there is inconsistency of treatment by government organisations. The Inland Revenue treat us as a charity for corporation tax and we do not get charged. However, HM Customs & Excise, who run VAT, do not treat us as charitable for charitable puposes. [Researchers' note: Almost all charities pay VAT in almost all circumstances: the correspondent makes a common error in supposing charities to be VAT relieved.] They regard independent schools as a business so we have to pay VAT on any sports facilities that we develop which are also available to local community. Independent schools do have difficulty fundraising locally. There is a prejudice against helping schools which are viewed as supported by rich parents. We, however, take many special needs children from the LEA because our special needs faciliites are better than those available on the state. The LEAs pay."

"The school itself is a charity – we raise considerable funds every year from grant-making charities to support bursaries for our pupils. We raise funds for development: we raise funds to give away. The responsibilities for this fundraising lie with a variety of people including the headmaster, governors, admin staff etc."

About being a special school

"As a special school, it is important that our pupils recognise that others have significant needs."

"Some of our parents live a considerable distance from the school and many have enough to do with looking after their child with severe learning disabilities; babysitting is very difficult for our parents because they need specialist helpers."

"We think it is important that our students don't just see themselves as recipients of others' giving."

"There are high costs of equipment for special schools, therefore we are constantly fundraising. Our pupils benefit greatly from the generous support of others, so we encourage pupils to reciprocate by raising funds for Children in Need or Comic Relief."

"Small schools such as ours, which deal with people with emotional and behavioural difficulties do not have socio-economic backgrounds which enable the school to generate self-help from within the parent-school partnership. The annual bid by the leading stores, to engage us in generating vouchers for resources, however, worthy, is not accessible to us. We cannot generate enough points etc from within the school base and we certainly do not appeal to the general public as a source for donations. Access for all, with equality of opportunity is the key."

About fundraising for charities and community causes

"Primary schools are bombarded with requests from charities to enter into competitions and sponsored events to raise funds for them. Firstly, we are here to educate children – not to ply them with competition entries. Secondly, we prefer to donate funds to our own local charities from the school, such as Harvest, Christmas, Poppy Day etc."

"If a cause is deemed to be of significant worthiness by the staff and students, we would consider raising money for it. We are less inclined to respond to the many requests via the school mail."

"Our school is located in an area of rural deprivation. The budget resources are quite good, so our fundraising is usually for extras or for charity. We sponsor a young girl in India through Action Aid."

"Charity fundraising is good for team-building and training in responsibility."

"We see it as integral to the ethos of the school. It is very much a part of our caring philosophy. Pupils also receive support from charities to participate in learning projects, which in turn raise money for other charities, e.g. Friends Provident, Barnardos, Barclays' Future Challenge."

About us

"Thankyou for a questionnaire that could be completed fairly painlessly!"

FINDINGS
POLICY ISSUES AND PROPOSALS

Rebuilding the consensus
For many years it was a central tenet of charity theory that charitable funding should not substitute for statutory funding – an increasingly important issue as the welfare state progressively took over what were originally regarded as charitable obligations in health care, in the relief of poverty and in education.

The need to define 'supplement'
In the case of education, this old assumption has become increasingly frayed at the edges in the last decade. There is no political consensus on what should be provided from public funds and what it is acceptable for a maintained school to raise money for externally. This is not only a question of identifying specific categories of expenditure which lie outside the expectation of statutory funding, but also a question of judging how far voluntary and other funding (whether by 'self-help' or by recourse to companies, trusts and similar sources) can or should 'top-up' perceived inadequacies in the amount of state funding. Though it was held that charitable funds should not substitute, they could supplement, but the distinction between the two is blurred if statutory funding is insufficient for present or new needs.

The need to allay fears of off-loading
Top-up funding carries risks. On the one hand, there are fears that government might pull back if voluntary sources are showing themselves willing to take some of the load. Moreover, some of those voluntary sources may tend to favour the haves rather than have-nots, the short-term over the long-term and the emotive not the unattractive. On the other hand, without such top-up funding, schools risk becoming too underprovided to meet their obligations, including those imposed by an increasingly regulatory government. This whole issue needs public debate (whether sponsored by the voluntary sector, LEAs or the DfEE) and policy guidance from central government.

The need for adequate funding
One consequence of the lack of consensus on this subject is that many maintained schools remain reluctant fundraisers, differing from other voluntary sector fundraisers by their uncertainty about how far they should be doing it, and how far they may be actually encouraging the government to expect top-up funding from voluntary sources. Schools, parents and all others with a concern for education should put all possible pressure on the government to provide schools with enough direct core funding to deliver its own targets for achievement – taking proper account of disadvantage and the circumstances of individual schools and areas. Extra-curricular fundraising should be just that: not an assumed component of maintained school budgets but raising support for items and projects outside that which must be adequately resourced by central and local government. Many schools have already pioneered imaginative projects of this kind with their own local communities.

Underprovision: the need for Hallmarked schools
One way forward would be for the government to establish the concept of a 'Hallmark' school (akin to a British Standard), which would define the minimum standard of premises, equipment, staffing (both numbers and qualifications) etc required to meet the needs of the relevant area and pupils. The aim would be that the government should be able not only to identify the schools that 'underperform' in terms of achievement (to which its main efforts now seem to be directed) but should also be able, preferably assisted by independent lay assessors, to identify those schools that are 'underprovided' to deliver that performance, or are failing to meet health and safety requirements.

That is not to revert to the old producer-led conviction that failure is entirely because of underfunding, but it is to assert that the school which is underprovided in relation to its pupils' needs is less likely to achieve the full potential of its pupils.

New guidance for funders

The Hallmark concept could be a guide for the optimal distribution of public funding (including such funds as SRB, NOF etc. as well as capital provision and more sophisticated formula funding of current budgets). It could also be a guide to voluntary funders like trusts and companies, whose efforts, however well-intentioned, are shown by this survey to be not always directed towards 'evening up'.

Companies and trusts: a new role?

Companies and trusts should be encouraged to review their policies to ensure that they are contributing to the achievement of equality of opportunity and raising the standards of lower achieving schools within their areas of benefit. One way they could do this is by directing their help to education not to individual schools but to educational innovation by establishing and funding new 'Education Trusts' of general educational benefit, for instance within a particular area, with specific objectives like educational research, ICT or library development. There is no equivalent in education to the medical research charities in the health sector, to which concerned members of the public can also contribute.

Special schools – a special case

Our supplementary survey on special schools revealed some of the particular difficulties of this sector, though the sample was not big enough to draw very authoritative conclusions. It is clear that the funding requirements of these schools place a particular priority on additional funding, especially for those schools whose pupils' emotional and behavioural needs do not attract widespread public support, or where wide catchment areas or residential units make it difficult to draw on parental support. The government, LEAs and other funders should pay particular attention to their needs. Companies might consider weighting promotional voucher schemes in favour of small and special schools.

Independent schools

Our supplementary survey of independent schools scratches the surface of a very large subject. Data is not always available in the same form as for maintained schools, which complicates comparison. It is, however, clear that the independent sector contains a large number of schools (perhaps especially those catering for minority religions or 'alternative' values) which are far from the public school stereotype. On the other hand it is also clear that a relatively small number of independent schools are able to raise very large sums indeed, largely from tax-relieved sources of one kind or another. Whilst cooperation between the sectors is to be welcomed, the tax benefits granted to the richest schools, particularly through trust donations or high levels of investment income, need review.

Parents and the community: a new focus?

An important consideration in headteachers' minds is the fostering of links between parents and the community generally, including business, and the school – a highly important objective for any school. The emphasis on fundraising has in practice helped to encourage some schools to build bridges to their parents and other stakeholders whom they previously held at arms' length. But focusing these links mainly on fundraising is not the most fruitful way of engaging parental and community involvement, and can lead to the social exclusion of parents who are unemployed or on low incomes. The contribution of time, by business as well as by parents, can be more valuable than cash, as a means of creating an active school community.

Many schools would do well to refocus their efforts by developing a broader approach to involving parents and other stakeholders, using fundraising as only one of many ways of attracting people to become involved with the school.

Teachers: new needs?

It is clear from the headteachers' comments quoted in this report that the burden of fundraising is a major one, and a significant distraction in terms of both effort and time from the principal educational role of teachers. Senior teachers might benefit from having training in volunteer management. Voluntary organisations may be a helpful source of advice and assistance with the development of focused, appropriate fundraising strategies and the preparation of applications and bids.

Accountability and transparency

The present arrangements for the accountability, regulation and transparency of charitable funds in schools remain a mess. The effect of transferring schools and their associated charities and other funds from the supervision of the Charity Commission to that of the DfEE, completed by the 1998 Education Act, creates a large gap in the system. Although many PTAs and HSAs are registered as charities with the Charity Commission (especially since the establishment of an income threshold for the regulation of small charities), the School Standards and Framework Act 1998 leaves it unclear whether or not some of them, like the schools they support, are now exempt. This needs clarification.

Better Regulation: a new 'Schools House'?

In principle, the DfEE's and the LEAs' general oversight of school accounts should extend to these funds; in practice they do not appear to do anything in this area, and both regulation (in the form of audit and inspection) and transparency (in the form of public availability of accounts) appear to be lacking. The Charity Commission and the DfEE should stop ducking this issue and consider how to fill the gap. One way would be to establish a 'Schools House' (akin to Companies House), where school accounts including the full extent, sources and use of school voluntary income could be made available for public scrutiny.

Parental covenants and Gift Aid

Parental covenants and Gift Aid donations to schools, widely used in the independent sector and in some of the high fundraising maintained sector schools, raise an important issue of charity and tax law. Charitable status is intended to exclude private benefit. That is clearly not the case with parental covenants to schools, where the pupils benefiting are the children of the donors. The government should review this important gap in current arrangements, particularly since recent changes to the regulation of tax-effective giving to charities is otherwise likely to lead to an increase in this form of support.

Information and training: a new need

Many schools described how they felt excluded, not only by the bureaucracy of grant and bid applications, but also because they did not always know where, how and how best to apply. Funders should consider simplifying forms and procedures. DfEE should also act to make sure schools have easier access to information and guidance on how to tap charitable and other sources of supplementary funding, possibly by electronic means.

School fundraising for other charities: a new understanding

Guidelines, notes and examples of good practice in charity fundraising in partnership with schools should be disseminated widely to charities looking to schools for support, and to the schools themselves. These should stress the need for the charity to understand the school, to create a genuine partnership for the delivery of the

National Curriculum, and to avoid placing unnecessary pressure on staff. A forum for discussion of the needs fo schools and the needs of charities would be a welcome development, particularly if supported by training and subsequent mutual support.

The new consensus

The issues in this short report highlight only one small corner of a much larger and more important challenge for education in the twenty first century: what is the relationship between underachievement by schools and underprovision by government? What is a fair funding mechanism for schools? How can society at large, and government in particular, ensure that all schools reach an acceptable standard of provision as well as of achievement? How can those of good will best support pupils, teachers and schools? And how can we prevent schools and pupils in poorer areas continuing to miss out?

The achievement of a new consensus about good practice in school fundraising could tap public willingness to support education through donations and, through the donation of time, as mentors, funders and friends. Schools of all kinds could take pride in the innovative projects that enriched school life and their local communities. Pupils would find themselves in fairer competition and headteachers could devote their time to the strategic planning, curriculum development and school leadership that encourages excellence. To achieve all this, we need leadership from government, and pressure from public and voluntary bodies. Above all, we need first to learn from the experience of schools.

INDEX

200 Club..................................23/39/52/62
affinity cards............................23/39/52/62
aims, survey...................................15
Arts Council...................................27/56
Arts Lottery Fund..........................27/43/65
Baring Foundation..............................9
bid culture, the.............................17/26/55
Charitable status.............................12/14
Charities Act 1960.............................13
Charities Act 1992.............................13
Charity Commission................7/12/13/14/77
City Academies.................................11
City Technology Colleges.....................9/12
community schools.............................24
community special schools....................14
companies................6/27/30/42/43/49/55/77
covenants..............................23/39/52/62/77
development appeal.........................23/39
Department for Education and Employment
    (DfEE)..........................7/13/15/75/77
Diocese...................................27/28/65
Directory of Social Change (DSC)...........9/15/50
disadvantage and deprivation..............29/45/57/66
Education Act 1993.............................13
Education Business Partnerships (EBP)........10/65
Education Reform Act 1988............11/12/13/77
Education Trusts................................7
excepted charities.............................12
exempt charities..............................12/14
foundation special schools....................14
governing bodies.............................13/14
free school meals..............................66
Friends' Association.........................26/64
GEST/Standards Fund............................5
Gift Aid..............................23/39/52/62/77
governors, school..............................15
grant maintained schools..................11/39/44
Hallmark school..............................6/75
Henley, Lord...................................13
Heritage Board (National Lottery)...............27
Home-School Association (HSA)....10/14/17/18/26/42/55/64
House of Lords................................13
independent schools
    charity and community causes, and..........50/58
    difficulties and information needs of........57
    factors affecting fundraising in..............57
    how fundraising is managed...................54
    how money is raised..........................52
    how much is raised by.......................5/51
    what money is raised for.....................52

Inland Revenue..................................14
Labour government...............................9
legacies................................23/39/52/62
Local Education Authority (LEA)............7/75/77
Millennium Fund (National Lottery)..............43
National Confederation of Parent-Teacher Associations
    (NCPTA)....................................10
National Curriculum, the.....................9/10
National Foundation for Educational Research (NFER).......16
National Lottery Charities Board................27
National Lottery..................6/15/27/43/56/65
New Opportunities Fund (NOF).......17/28/44/57/65/76
Parent-Teacher Association (PTA).....10/14/17/18/26/42/55/64
primary schools
    charity and community causes, and.........5/33/34
    difficulties and information needs of........31
    factors affecting fundraising in..............19
    how fundraising is managed...................24
    how money is raised..........................22
    how much is raised by.......................19/21
    what money is raised for resources manager...21
rural area..................................20/29
School Fund....................................41
School Standards and Framework Act 1998......13/14
Schools House, establishment of..............7/77
secondary schools
    charity and community causes, and............47
    difficulties and information needs of........66
    factors affecting fundraising in..............44
    how fundraising is managed................40/41
    how money is raised..........................38
    how much is raised by....................5/35/37
    what money is raised for.....................52
Secretary of State for Education................15
special schools
    charity and community causes, and.........5/60/67
    difficulties and information needs of........66
    factors affecting fundraising in..............59
    how fundraising is managed.................63/64
    how money is raised........................62/63
    how much is raised by......................59/61
    what money is raised for...................61/62
Single Regeneration Budget (SRB)............43/70/76
sponsorship..................................23/39
tax-effective giving..........................23/39/52
trading......................................23/39/55
trusts, charitable..........6/27/30/32/42/43/49/55/56/77
urban, areas....................................20
voluntary schools..............................14
    aided......................................6/24
    controlled...................................24

79

Acronyms

CTC	City Technology College
DfEE	Department for Education and Employment
DSC	Directory of Social Change
GM	Grant-maintained (school)
EBP	Education Business Partnership
GEST	Grants for Education Support and Training
HSA	Home–School Association
ICT	Information and Communication Technology
LEA	Local Education Authority
LMS	Local Management of Schools
NCPTA	National Confederation of Parent–Teacher Associations
NFER	National Foundation for Educational Research
NOF	New Opportunities Fund
PTA	Parent–Teacher Association
SRB	Single Regeneration Budget
TEC	Training and Enterprise Councils

Areas used in the survey

In the Primary School Findings:

Area A/r is a rural area in the south of England

Area B/r is a rural area in the east of England

Area C/u is an urban area in the west of England

Area D/u is an urban area in the north of England